STICKY SITUATIONS

Understanding the Law and Life Skills

BY KRYSTAL BANKS

STICKY SITUATION

Understanding the Law and Life Skills

BY KRYSTAL BANKS

ISBN: 978-1-7334072-0-5

Cover Design by:	Lauren Williams
Edited by:	Gloria Palmer (movinonup57@yahoo.com)
First Printing:	August 2019
Second Printing:	May 2020
Third Printing:	September 2021

This Book belongs to:

Name: ______________________________ **Age:** _____

Table of Contents

1. Introduction

Juveniles don't understand that the decisions you make as minors can affect your lives forever. We know everyone makes mistakes. We are all constantly changing. That's why we don't keep the same friends. People change and grow and go in different paths in life, and it is important to make the right choices. You won't always get a chance to start over, especially with the law and your record.

Young people need to understand, when you make certain choices, it can change your whole life. For example, if you chose to steal something, people won't trust you. This can cause you to stop trusting people and to think everyone is out to get you. It isn't a good mindset to have—worrying. Who wants to live a life always looking over your shoulder?

Sometimes, when you're a minor and you get in trouble with the law, you can get a second chance. When I say second chance, I mean, in the juvenile system, most charges won't go on your permanent record. For example, the first time you have a fight, the juvenile court may let it slide, but the second time around, they won't. What you may not know is there are some cases that stay on your record and you won't be able to remove them. Then, when you become an adult and have issues, you will have to try to get the charge expunged off your record.

When you apply to go to college or to get loans and grants, juvenile charges can come up on your record. You may not be able to get a job if you have a record. Criminal records and credit are very important in life. If you mess them up, when you're ready to do what you want, they can stop you and make your life so much harder than it should be. In some cases, you may get the opportunity to clear the charges off your record. That's called getting an Expungement.

When you don't do what your parents tell you to do, you get punished. Many parents punish their children by taking away their possessions, yelling, or perhaps, spankings. But the reality is, children have no idea what the real world is like. Discipline is needed because it helps prepare you for the future.

The fact is, people don't always think they are committing a crime, and they don't always get caught doing that crime at that time. The fact that they didn't get caught doesn't make it right. This book is to show you how easy it is to break the law, especially when you didn't know it was a crime. You were just having fun, but fun can quickly turn into trouble. This Workbook is to help teach you to stop and think—instead of getting in trouble. The jail and prison populations are growing. Posting bail for minors is becoming more common.

You want to understand life's situations and how the system works before you do anything wrong and find yourself in this type of situation. ***YOU DON'T WANT TO FIND OUT***

THE HARD WAY. That's why it is so important to have these conversations with your parents and teachers.

Don't wait until you get into trouble to try to understand what's going on with your situation. You need to know before it happens how it's going to go because, in the system, you will have to depend on and trust attorneys and people you don't know to look out for you and help you. With this type of book, at least you'll be able to understand what's going on because a lot of attorneys won't have time to explain to you all that's going on with you and your case.

❖❖❖

2. Know Your Rights

A. Rights That Apply To Minors

Minors do have legal rights. You have the right to equal protection. You have the right to due process, to have your day in court, an education, basic needs, health care, good nutrition, and a safe environment.

(1) The 1st Amendment. Freedom of Speech, Religion, Press, Assembly & Petition.

You have the right to:

- Say what you want without causing a dangerous situation.
- Believe in whatever religion you want—or don't believe in one at all—your choice.
- Write what you want, just not on other people's property.
- Disagree with the government and sue them.

There are rules on freedom of speech. For example, you can't yell something like fire in a public place because it could cause people to panic, causing a dangerous situation.

(a) If the police stop you and ask you a question, do you have to answer? If so, what do you have to tell them?

____

____

____

(b) What can happen if you curse at the police?

(c) Do you have to pray or stand for the national anthem (in schools or in public)?

(d) Can you write or draw on anything, anywhere?

(e) Do you have the right to hang out in a group?

(f) Do you have the right to not like a rule the government makes?

(g) What's the procedure to try to change the rules without getting punished by the government?

(h) Can a minor sue the government?

(i) Can you get sued as a minor?

(2) The 2nd Amendment. The Right to Bear Arms

If you are of legal age, you have the right to have a weapon and use it to protect yourself.

(a) Can you carry a weapon just to protect yourself? If so, what kind of weapon?

____

____

____

(3) The 4th Amendment. Search and Seizure

The government cannot arrest you or search your property unless they have Probable Cause.

Probable Cause: The police think you have committed a crime or have some type of criminal evidence. It means you are 51% more likely to have done something wrong.

Probable Cause needed for a minor: The police can only search you if they suspect you have violated a criminal statue. However, public officials, like school staff, only need to think you have done something related to a crime.

For example: You keep leaving class, and every time you come back to class, you're acting funny—like you're high or drunk. Then they can pat you down and search your locker.

(a) If you let the police in your house, can they search it?

____

____

(b) Do you have the right to a phone call? If so, who should you call?

____

____

(c) Can cellphones accept collect calls?

____

(4) The 5th Amendment. The Right To Not Self-Incriminate.

If you are a minor, you probably think the police can't question you without a parent or legal guardian present. But, if they ask you questions, it is up to you to remain silent. If you think it's just questions and answers, understand that the police will let you talk, and yes, they can and will use everything you are saying against you.

(a) What are Miranda rights and does a minor have Miranda rights?

____

____

____

____

____

(b) When should you ask for an attorney—while you're being arrested or after you've been detained?

____

____

(c) If the police ignore your request for your parents and attorney, can they keep questioning you? What do you do next?

____

____

____

(d) If the police don't tell you your Miranda rights, can you escape punishment?

____

(e) What is the number one rule when dealing with the police?

____

3. Do You Really Know What Jail Is Like?

Describe what you think jail is really like. What do you think it looks like inside a cell?

____

____

____

____

____

____

____

____

✸✸✸

You're trapped in a building with strangers who won't let you use the phone, watch television, play video games, use a computer, exercise, or just hang out and do what you want. You get a small bed with a toilet and a sink, and you have to share that space with someone who may be nasty. They may not like to clean. They may be rude and not care about anything. You are in a cell that is 6 feet by 8 feet. You have to go to the bathroom in front of each other all the time. *You get **NO** privacy.* You have no clue if the other person in your cell is crazy or has mental issues, but you're stuck with them as a cellmate. Then, 3 times a day, you get to eat some nasty food—things like boiled eggs, dry bread, milk, bread and bologna with no mayo or mustard, maybe some old fruit and vegetables, and dinner that looks like dog food.

NOW WHAT DO YOU THINK JAIL IS LIKE?

✸✸✸

THE GOVERNMENT JUST PASSED A NEW NET NEUTRALITY LAW WHERE THEY NOW CONTROL THE INTERNET. SO, IF THEY DON'T LIKE WHAT YOU'RE SAYING OR POSTING ON SOCIAL MEDIA, THEY CAN BLOCK IT! NOW, YOU ARE GOING TO HAVE TO BUY A BOOK OR DOWNLOAD ONE TO FIND OUT THE TRUTH. ONE OF YOUR FREEDOMS OF SPEECH JUST GOT TAKEN AWAY! THERE'LL BE NO MORE GETTING RICH OFF DUMB STUFF ON SOCIAL MEDIA BECAUSE THE GOVERNMENT WILL BE CONTROLLING THE MONEY YOU USE TO BE ABLE TO MAKE OFF YOUR POSTS OR VIDEOS GOING VIRAL! DO YOU UNDERSTAND, SINCE IT IS NOW A LAW, IF YOU BREAK IT, IT IS A CRIME? THIS IS WHY YOU NEED TO KNOW HOW A BILL BECOMES A LAW. GOOGLE: SCHOOLHOUSE ROCK (AMERICA, I'M JUST A BILL).

4. Workbook Questionnaire

1. What do you think jail is like?
   a. A clean room where you hang out and watch television.
   b. An area where you sit in a room and watch television.
   c. A dirty room where there is a bed, a toilet, and a small sink.

2. Who do you think cleans the jail?
   a. Staff
   b. Yourself
   c. Janitor

3. How much free time daily do you think you get to have in jail?
   a. 4 hours
   b. 2 hours
   c. 1 hour

4. What do you think you get when you're in jail? *(circle all you think apply)*
   a. Television
   b. Radio
   c. Computer
   d. iPad/iPod
   e. School time
   f, Snacks
   g. Nice clothes
   h. Phone
   i. Books
   j. Paper and pencil
   k. Gym
   l. Video games
   m. Blanket
   n. Pillow
   o. Soap and deodorant
   p. Washcloths
   q. Toothpaste/toothbrush
   r. Couch
   s. Hair care products
   t. Bed

5. What type of programs do you think they teach you in jail? *(circle all the ones you think apply)*
   a. Math
   b. English
   c. Social studies
   d. Arts
   e. Music
   f. Science
   g. Reading
   h. Computers

6. How do you pick out your clothes in jail?
   a. Small store
   b. Catalog
   c. Uniform

7. Do you have open access to the refrigerator and snack areas in jail?
   a. All day
   b. 4 hours a day
   c. Never

8. Are you safer in jail or out of jail? ____________

9. Does a minor have to have identification? ____________

10. How old does a minor have to be to get an identification card? ____________

11. What do you think your rights are as a minor?

____

____

____

____

12. Can the police question you without your parents or your legal guardian? Why or why not?

____

____

____

____

____

13. Is it illegal to send, share, or repost nude pictures of yourself on Facebook or on a cellphone?

____

____

____

14. Can you get in trouble for being with someone who breaks the law?

____

15. Do you have to give the police your name and ID if you are a passenger? Can they search you as a passenger?

____

____

____

5. *Better Choices*

With the law, you get into more trouble by what you do, not by what you wanted to do. What that means is, if you break the law but you weren't trying to hurt someone, it's less of a crime. But, if it's a violent act, you are going to get into more trouble. The fact that you didn't intend on hurting someone does not excuse the fact that a crime has been committed, and you will be punished for the crime. Not knowing the law does not prevent punishment.

DON'T TAKE ANY CRIME LIGHTLY. A CRIME IS A CRIME—BIG OR SMALL. You may commit a crime and it doesn't seem like a big deal, but you still are committing a crime. So, don't just ignore it! You must take it seriously! People do crimes—everyday things—like use their parents' debit cards. Even though your parents gave you permission, it is still breaking the law. You can't get mad when you get charged with a felony. The court doesn't care if you do it all the time and you don't think it's a big deal. It will be when you have to pay attorney fees, bail, and court fines!

If you want to steal a car, the way you steal it can be the difference between 2 years in jail and life in jail. If you threaten someone while you are stealing the car makes the charges worse.

- Carjacking is the threat of a person, a 25-year offense.

vs.

Unlawful Driving Away Automobile (UDAA): breaking a window and stealing a car or snatching the keys and stealing a car.

- Armed Robbery: you don't have to have a weapon to actually be charged with armed robbery. All you have to do is take money from a person who didn't want to give you the money.

Carjacking: life in prison, 25 years Threat of a person, stealing a car	*vs*	Unlawful Driving Away Automobile (UDAA): 2+ yrs. Same outcome—you stole a car
If you knew the difference between carjacking and stealing a car, would you throw your life away? You would be better off snatching the keys and running, or busting out a window and stealing the car, because if you say anything, it crosses the line to a threat, and that's a life offense.		
Armed Robbery: life Threat and taking an item on a person	*vs*	Larceny: 93 days-10 yrs. Taking an item (not on a person)

Driving without a license (DWL) You had a license, but you lost it and you can't drive until you fix what the State wants you to fix to get it back.	*VS*	Not having a license: You and the owner of the vehicle will both get in trouble because if you never had a license you can't drive, and you can't let someone drive without them having a license.

One of the worst things that can happen to minors is they get lied to and tricked by adult criminals. Criminals say: You won't get in trouble or charged as an adult. *That's a lie!* They say: When you do get charged, you aren't going to get into real trouble because you're a minor. *That's a lie!* What they won't tell you is: You will go to jail, and if you are old enough, you will be transferred to an adult jail. Juveniles have a juvenile jail and juvenile prison, but you still go to some type of jail. It is not like what you see on television.

The reason these criminals act like they're your friend is because they *know* they'll get in trouble for the crime and they will go to jail, so they set kids up who don't know any better. ***DON'T GET PLAYED!***

Most charges stay on your juvenile record, but some can also stay on your permanent adult record. Then you will have to try to get it expunged just like an adult because you will not get approved for a loan, grants, jobs, or scholarship with a record.

The things you see in the streets are not always what they seem to be. What I mean is, just because someone is driving a nice car and dresses nice doesn't always mean it is real. Lots of people lie and fake it. People rent cars, homes, jewelry, and clothes, and now there is even lay-a-way on hair, so don't be fooled. We want you to understand that getting a job and building your credit is more important that what looks good. What looks good is a good credit score, owning your own home, paying your bills on time, and having no debt. Start small and get bigger so you don't get played by the system. When I say this, I mean, everyone is going to have to get a job to take care of themselves. You can stay fresh and lease a new car, and even rent a nice apartment, but none of that is owning. It's what you do with your money that will help you.

You're better off saving your money and buying a small house. For example, save $10,000, buy a house for $5,000, and use $5,000 to renovate it, so you can own it. Then, when you need money, you can use it as collateral to borrow money. You can do that process over again, then you'll have something to start with, rather than keep paying rent to someone else who owns where you are staying. That's making them money and throwing yours away. Did you know, at age 13, you can put money in a special account, and when you turn 18, you can take that money out and use it to buy your first home without interest? And all you have to do is put $210 in a certificate of deposit (CD) account or a money market account every month for 4 years. This is knowing what to do with your money. The same with a car. It's better to pay cash for your car and have it fully insured with extra insurance than to lease something just to look good. Then, if something goes wrong, you won't be fixing someone else's car that, when your lease is up, you have to give back to them.

Once you buy the house, you have to live in it or get a renter. Just know, when you get the tenant, you must have a contract (lease), so if they damage your house, you can go after them. Then, you'll need your own insurance on the house to protect your investment. When you figure out how much rent you're going to charge, make sure you include your taxes, which are due at the end of the year, so you don't lose your home you worked so hard for.

And last, but not least, if you rent your house out, you need to take the money you collect for rent and put 70% of the money in a savings account for any repairs that may be necessary or so you can buy another house in about 2 years. If you don't touch the money and keep flipping houses, you will make a lot of money. Or you can invest some of your savings, about thirty percent, into the stock market. You would own a piece of that business, and if they make money, so do you. If you like Nike, buy some stock in Nike, so every time they make money, so do you. It's called making your money work for you.

For example: If you buy fifty shares of a stock for $15 per share, that's an investment of $750. After 2 years, if the stock price increases to $20, your investment is now worth $1,000. This is before any fees and commissions are taken out. Just sitting in a savings account, you won't make $250 worth of interest in 2 years. This is why understanding money is important and you can do it as a young person. It's making your money work for you, instead of wasting money on things that won't help you. You need to invest in companies that are constantly making money. But if you see the company isn't making money, take your money out. You aren't in the business of losing money. To take money out, you have to sell shares equal to the amount of money you want to take out. The stock game is better played keeping your money in a company for years, not by taking it in and out.

When it comes to building and starting your own business, use your money wisely. If you save $300, get a prepaid debit card, go online, and buy weave bundles wholesale, then flip them for 4 times the amount. *For example:* you buy 25 bundles for $300, but you sell each bundle for $40 apiece. You will make $1,000. That's a $700 profit. Then you re-order, but maybe get 50 bundles next time, and keep making your money. That's being a boss not a worker. Once you start making a profit, make sure you start a savings account. You should save 25-50% of what's left of your profit after you re-invest in your product.

This beats the quick-money game of things like selling drugs. At least you can see your money working, and you don't have to worry about watching your back or you're doing something illegal. Drugs tend to end up being a long-term plan with no benefits. You get a line of credit with a dealer, which puts your butt on the line to make a little money, when you could invest a little bit of money and watch it grow over time. When you invest, what you're doing is buying a piece of the company. Imagine having stock in Jordan shoes, then you notice all your friends wearing them. Guess what? You're making money off them buying shoes from a company that you are partial owner.

The system is built to make money, where you are in debt. They never tell you, if you lose your job and you're in a lot of debt, you could lose everything. When it comes to dressing, you need to think about when you see a homeless person. You may think, yuck, and you don't want to touch them because of how they look. Well, when you think you're dressing cool, most people with money, good jobs, and sense think yuck about you wearing your pants down off your butt or not combing your hair. You look sloppy to them, like you don't care about yourself. Or, if you wear tight or low-cut clothes, maybe with some type of holes or cut-outs in them, you think you look cute, but you look a hot mess. A real professional wouldn't wear that. They would have on a nice blouse and skirt, or a nice shirt and slacks. It doesn't take a lot of money to look nice. You may laugh, but you won't get the job.

I tell you all of this so you can understand that everything makes a difference when people are looking at you, no matter if it's in the court, on a job, or you're just trying to impress the right person. You need to have your stuff together. Everyone isn't going to go to college or going to be rich, but you have to learn how to take care of yourself no matter what. You can look at someone like the garbage man, who has unlimited overtime and probably no degree, but he makes just as much money as an engineer without the debt of paying back college tuition.

DON'T LET JOB TITLES FOOL YOU! THERE IS A LOT OF MONEY TO BE MADE.

If you find out someone—even if it's a parent—has used your name and social security number to put a bill in your name, then they didn't pay it, people will tell you that you need to charge them with a crime to get it off your credit. No, you don't. You just need to prove to the credit bureau it wasn't you. If you were underage, prove to them you were a minor, so they can remove it from your credit report.

A. Misdemeanor Vs. Felony

Felonies and some misdemeanors stay on your permanent record. They will not automatically fall off your record. It isn't like your credit report, where things fall off after 7-10 years. You can have some things removed after 3 years for a misdemeanor and 5 years for a felony. Removal from your record is called Expungement. You can do Expungements yourself, but most hire attorneys because it's easier.

Expungement is the process to remove a misdemeanor or a felony from your record. Getting an Expungement is a privilege, *not a right. That means they don't have to remove it.*

(1) Misdemeanor

A misdemeanor is a minor crime punishable by a fine and/or county jail time for up to 1 year. It is handled in the lower courts, such as Municipal, Justice, or District Court. Misdemeanor punishment is county jail time, not prison. Misdemeanors don't always show up on your criminal background record.

Typical misdemeanors include: petty theft, simple assault and battery, disturbing the peace, drunk driving without injury to others, drunkenness in public, various traffic violations, public nuisances, and some crimes which can be charged as either a felony or a misdemeanor, depending on the circumstances and the discretion of the district attorney.

(2) Felony

A felony is a charge where you get punished for a minimum of 1 year and 1 day, sending you to prison. A felony means a violation of a penal law of this state, for which the offender, upon conviction, may be punished by death or by imprisonment for more than one year, or an offense expressly designated by law to be a felony.

A charge is considered a felony if the offense was punishable by more than one year of incarceration, or, when the statutory penalty is not available, if the crime was designated as a felony in the convicting jurisdiction at the time of a prior conviction.

If you have more than one felony, you may have to work harder to remove some items from your criminal record. You may have to see if you qualify for the *Proxy Nunc Pro Tunc*—that's where you can go back in time and change your conviction to perhaps a lesser conviction, taking it down to a misdemeanor. It falls under the interest of justice.

You must get things removed from your criminal record or they will be on your record forever. In some cases, it can't be removed. *For example,* if you have 2 felonies or you have a drunk driving conviction.

B. Simple To Serious

Just because you don't *think* you break the law doesn't mean you don't. As a young person, you may not be aware of all the laws you break and the repercussions to them. But how can people expect you to know without teaching you?

For example: You go to your friend's house and leave your clothes or your Xbox over there, or you let them borrow your clothes or Xbox. Somehow, they destroy them—whether it was an accident, or they burnt them up, or bleached them, or they got mad at you and threw them away, or just broke it—these are crimes. If someone damages or destroys your property, it is called malicious destruction of property. Depending on how much the property costs, it could be a misdemeanor or a felony. And you have the right to sue them for the damages and press charges against them. So, if your friend borrowed your Xbox and broke it, and it cost $700, you can sue them for $1,000 or more, and put them in jail.

There are some activities you may not know are illegal or may not have started out as illegal. *For example:* You have a video game you play, but you short cut it and look up some codes on Google or YouTube to skip levels. There's nothing wrong with this. Now, you get a new phone and you want to get games on your phone, then you realize you need a credit card to purchase these games and you don't have one, so you look up how to jailbreak your phone. It's just putting a code in your phone to override the system so the games you want are free, right? Wrong! *It is stealing, and it is illegal.* Just like with a firestick. It isn't illegal until you jailbreak it. Just think of the word *jailbreak*. There is nothing good about this word! Most systems are not meant to be altered.

C. How People Judge You

It starts very early in life. *For example:* If you are a student who doesn't pay attention, doesn't do your homework, makes excuses, and maybe is the class clown, you may not see this is setting you up for some problems. Every student has his or her own file. It is called your permanent record. This is where your teachers can put a note about you so the next teacher can know how to deal with you. This file can even be referred to when you're an adult and have had some problems. They can pull these files out up to five years after you reach adulthood. You may think it isn't a big deal, but you are building a reputation that will be used against you when you do finally grow up and try to do something with yourself.

When you get to be a little older, let's say maybe high school, you will have even more profiling going on: people watching what you wear, how you style your hair, your temper and attitude. If you are trying to better yourself in life or just trying to get by, they are taking notes. This can determine if they think you going down the wrong path. You may need to talk to an adult and be real with them. Ask them what they think of you and where they see your future going. What they tell you may shock you.

The point of telling you this is some people expect you to know this, but this book is here to explain what you may not know and how it applies to your life now and later. Every choice you make always has consequences—some good, some bad. This book is not going to sugarcoat what the real world is like. It is to prepare you to work hard, so your life can work out for you.

Then you have profiling about who you hang out with: Are they good kids? Do they make good choices? Are they going to be messed up in life? You may not see it yet, but a lot of times your parents do and that's why they don't want you hanging with them. Your parents may not want you hanging out with certain friends just to be mean, but because they see something you don't see. See, because you are their friends, you think they'll have your back, but what you may not know is your parents know their type—they have always been a snake—but your parents don't want to tell you this. Or you *friend* has some sneaky ways you may not be aware of that can get you caught up in some mess, but you won't be able to see it because you're too close to it.

You should pay attention to your surroundings at all times. If you're in an area you aren't familiar with, pay particular attention. You don't want to be the person who gets shot because you thought it *looked* safe. It's also a part of profiling. Keep your guard up at all times! It can save your life. Be smart! When something looks like it's about to get dangerous, ***GET AWAY!***

Then there is police profiling. These police may not be from where you're from. They look at your style and assume you don't care about yourself or your parents don't care about you because they let you walk around looking crazy. They assume your parents may not be crap because people who "have sense" wouldn't allow their children to go out like that, so they pick on you. They think you're a troublemaker, or you're so ignorant, you don't know your rights.

Maybe your parents didn't know any better and didn't teach you to do your hair, or put on a belt, or wear clothes that fit so other people won't misjudge you or treat you bad. You will find in life people are always judging you, but it's up to you to get them to see what you're really about. Know that may mean you have to be smart enough to play the role. Play the role means you may have to change a little to get what you want out of the situation. There is a time and place for everything. You won't see any famous people going to meet someone important looking like a bum. They put their best outfit together to meet the important people. It's like, if you look clean, like you're respectable, people will approach you differently. They will be more prone to listen to you and maybe even hire you. But, if you look like a slob, you won't get anywhere. You need to get the job first; then, if you want to change your style, you can. Think about it: If you were lost, would you ask a bum on the street for directions? Or, would you ask someone who looks decent and neat?

D. Judged By The Company You Keep

This is why it is so extremely important to make good choices at an early age. Also, don't be a follower! Do things because you want to do them because you're the one who is going to have to deal with the consequences—good or bad.

For example: You're with your friends and one of them breaks the law. It's called guilt by association. That's when you are just as guilty as the one who committed the crime because you didn't have enough sense to walk away, stop them, or tell on them. And you'd best believe, the one who *snitches* or makes the first deal, gets off or gets a lighter sentence. ***DON'T EXPECT ANY LOYALTY WHEN IT'S YOU OR THEM.*** There is always someone trying to get out of it.

Young people, you need to understand there is a better way of fighting people than physically. It's by hitting them in their pockets. Imagine if someone hit you, but instead of beating them up, you sued them for hitting you, for let's say, five hundred dollars. I bet they and their parents wouldn't keep fighting you because it isn't worth it. See, if they don't pay, you can collect items from them—like, take their TV or computers out their house, or even their car. You make them pay until they won't do it again. It's a money game. In life, you need it, but it's how you use it that makes the difference.

E. Having The Skills To Survive

Young people need to understand you can make your own money and can set yourself up to make money early in life. You do not always need a college education to get a good job and make good money. College is great, but it isn't for everyone. As a young person, you can find jobs like babysitting, cutting grass, shoveling snow, doing hair, and many other jobs. You can do an apprenticeship program or an intern program, which is when a company will train you to do a job.

For example: If you know a plumber, a mechanic, or an electrician, you can learn what they are doing so, one day, you can service people too. Just getting a skill like this, you will always have a job. This doesn't mean you won't have to get some type of education or training for this job later. You may need some type of certificate, but that is later down the road.

You need to remember you always need a skill to survive. The way you should look at life and having skills is easy: If you are at home and your furnace goes out, you will call around to find the fastest person who can fix it. If it's really cold out, some people won't care if they have a license or not, as long as they get the job done. That is called job stability. So, if you know how to fix the furnace, you'll have a job for life, and these types of people make a lot of money and fast. And they didn't have to spend thousands of dollars for a college degree, so remember to never look down on people with skills because they can save you when you need them. Believe it or not, these people can make just as much money as lawyers and engineers, so don't knock their hustle.

When it comes down to making money and investing money, you need to think about what you're into. If it's fashion, hair weaves (bundles), makeup, or video games, it's all an investment, and when people buy it, it's putting money into your pocket, so even as a kid, you can be your own boss and become an entrepreneur.

F. Getting Justice

Everyone has a boss, so don't be afraid to go over their heads to make a complaint or a report. Make sure you keep records of it because you can't let people just get over on you. Things like if a teacher is picking on you. You can have the school remove you from that class. Put it on their record. Keep filing complaints. Eventually, it will come out in your favor. If you build a case, someone will have to listen, even if you have to take it to the Board of Education. Go on their social media account and make a complaint. Give them low ratings on Google or the Yellow Pages. Tell your story on social media, but don't bash them because you don't want them to come back on you. Know the right and wrong way to handle situations.

In court, if you feel your lawyer did you wrong, make a complaint with the Attorney Grievance Committee. If the judge isn't fair, make a complaint to the Judicial Tenure Committee about them. If your boss is treating you badly or not giving you a raise, go to corporate and file a complaint. There may be others with the same complaints and you can go after them. Just like they messed you over, you can mess them up too.

G. Check Yourself

For some reason, young people seem to think people have to be honest and nice to them. ***WRONG!*** You get what you give. You cannot have a bad attitude or be a smart mouth to others and think they have to take it from you. Even if you're having a bad day, you need to suck it up because you need to be able to see when people are trying to help you. If you have a bad attitude with someone for no reason, that can be the reason they won't go out of their way to help you. ***IF YOU WANT RESPECT, GIVE RESPECT! DON'T LET YOUR FEELINGS GET IN THE WAY!*** Learn how to get what you want in life by doing things the easy way. Don't let people knock you off your game, causing you to miss your opportunity because you were being a jerk. Outsmart them!

H. Responsibilities Of A Citizen

As a good citizen, you need to always tell the truth. A person's honesty is all they have when dealing with the judicial system. Some people are never taught how to do the right thing by telling the truth. They have this idea that they need to mind their own business, and if they keep their mouths shut, it will be okay. The truth is, when something happens to your family, you would want someone to tell what happened, right? Therefore, if you know someone committed a crime, you should tell them to turn themselves in.

I. If You Weren't Taught About Right And Wrong—Stopping The Vicious Cycle

Your natural instinct is to survive, to take what you want and need to survive. But what if no one ever told you what you were doing was wrong? What if no one ever taught you basic survival skills that could change your outcome, skills as simple as fishing so you won't starve? Then you could fish and perhaps sell your fish to make money to survive.

When it comes to the vicious cycle, you have to know right from wrong, and hopefully, someone cares about you enough to tell you when you are doing something wrong. Unfortunately, the government has created so many rules that instinct now can be a crime.

I have a seminar and webinars that I do that address many of the issues in this book. Some of the topics discussed are:

- Knowing and understanding the top reasons people get pulled over
- Why and how people get arrested when they're pulled over

- What flags an officer when they are typing up random plates
- How to not get illegally searched

The purpose of the seminars is to discuss issues that people may need extra help in understanding and communicating, with questions and answers.

❖❖❖

6. *Setting And Achieving Goals*

What do you want in your life and do you know how to get it?

Your parents' job is to get you prepared to leave home. Some parents handicap their children by letting them stay in their home because they are not ready to let them go. Or, they are afraid to let them grow up and go through what they went through. It is wrong for your parents to hold you back. For 18 years, it is their job to get you ready. You cannot live at home forever. You cannot *not* have a job or pay bills. Actually, you should be working by age 14 and paying at least one small bill to prepare you for leaving home.

Do you know why you need a job? You need a job to make money so you can survive. Who wants to live with their parents forever? The goal is to move out, work, and live your best life! There is a problem with the expectations of youths. They are so comfortable that they don't mind staying with their parents. Being motivated to accomplish things like getting your first job, going to college or a trade school, moving out of your parents' home, or buying your first car, then buying your first home are great accomplishments in your life. One of the greatest endeavors of life is navigating adulthood, and defining and charting your course. Don't you want to better yourself? When you watch television and see how and where people live, do you ever wonder how they got there? They work hard to move into the safest areas to raise their family. They make good decisions financially so they can continue to grow their wealth. There should come a time in your life when you look around and say, "I can and I want to do better." If you want to stay in the slums/the hood, it is your choice. It is also your choice if you want to get out of the situation you are in.

Understanding the importance of setting goals and achieving them is the difference between people who are wealthy and people who are not. In order to control your situation, you need to know why you are in it, what is the plan to get out of it, and put a timeline together to execute it. This is why it is important to pay attention to how people get what they want in life. Many people don't ask the necessary questions to improve their situation. It is not just about how do you get that, but it's also about what do you need to do to prepare yourself to get what everyone needs: credentials. You can look good, but does your portfolio prove it? Or, are you just faking it on the outside? Make a plan and complete it, even if you have to try multiple times. No one can stop you but you.

In life, there are certain steps you must take to progress. During these steps, you need to know why you are taking them and what can happen if you mess them up. For instance, do you know why you need a bank account and the importance of continuing a good relationship with a bank? In today's time, you will and can have a hard time cashing a check without a bank account. Yes, you can go to a convenience store, but they will charge you extra fees to give you your money. Is that right? No. You also must protect yourself when you have a bank account. There are people who do scams, like asking a young person to cash a check for them in their account. But maybe it's a bad check, or did you ever think why they would need you to deposit money into your account when that person is willing to split the money with you?

When other people try to use your banking information, it should be a red flag. Something is wrong with them doing their own banking. Maybe they are doing the old college scam of having you apply for student loans. The school gives you the money in your name, hoping you will use it for college, but you use that money for something else. The problem with that is the loan is in your name, and yes, you will have to pay it back eventually or it will cause problems on your credit, but you didn't think it through. You thought someone was hooking you up with how to get some quick cash, then you had the nerve to give them some of your money. Shaking my head! They played you. Why do they deserve your money? They don't.

Having a good relationship with a bank is everything, and it is another form of identification. Banks and credit unions talk to each other, just like law enforcement. They all have systems that talk to each other. You may be able to get away with something a few times, but eventually, it will catch up with you. Once you write or cash a bad check, or even worse overdraft your accounts and don't pay the banks back, they put you in a check system that eventually will let all financial establishments know you're a fraud and bad payer. Then, later in life, when you clean yourself up, you won't be able to get loans, mortgages, or buy a new car because you've been flagged.

There's also the right way to set up a proper business. Go to the State's website. Register your company's name. Apply for your Tax Identification Number, that's your business' social insurance number so the government can keep track of your business. Get insurances to cover you and your company. Set up your websites to promote yourself. And, get good ratings for your company because, yes, there's business credit as well.

Everything you do can help you as a person, especially a business person, but you have to know some of the steps to get to the next level in life. Most riches don't come overnight. It takes time and hard work. All this information leads up to you understanding money and credit because this information is connected to your credit.

7. Understanding Money

A. What Is Credit?

Credit is the ability for you to use borrowed money to obtain goods or services, based on your word and trust that payment will be made in the future.

B. How Does Credit Work?

Your credit rating score can range from 300 to 850, the higher the number the better. It is like in school: if you work hard and get good grades, people trust you more. It's a grading scale based on:

1. **Payment History**, shows if you pay your bills on time. (Late payments have a drastic negative effect.)

2. **Account Balances,** the amount of money used every month by the due date. (You should only use a 30% utilization ratio by the closing date.)

   For example: Your credit card limit is $10,000, and the payment is due on the 10th of every month. You must pay that card down to under $3,000 and you cannot use that card again until the closing date on the 14th if you want good credit. You should create a chart like the one below to keep track of your credit card debt.

Credit Card Debt Chart

Creditor/Account Name	Total Amount Owed	Credit Limit or Original Amount Owed	Debt-to-Credit Utilization (30%) (Credit Cards Only)	Minimum Monthly Payment	Interest Rate	Annual Fees	Date to Pay in Full to Pay No Interest	Due Date	Statement Closing Date	Target Date to Pay Off	Date Paid Off
Example:											
Discover Card	$1,300.00	$10,000.00	$3,000.00	$25.00	13.99%	$181.87	9th of the month	10th of the month	14th of the month		
Totals:	**$1,300.00**	**$10,000.00**	**$3,000.00**	**$25.00**	**N/A**	**$181.87**	**N/A**	**N/A**	**N/A**	**N/A**	**N/A**

3. **Credit History,** how long you have had an account. (Always keep the account open.)

4. **Variation of Credit Accounts,** that is the difference in installment and revolving credit accounts.

5. **Installment Payments,** payments you make on a loan until it is paid off (mortgage, auto loan, personal loan, etc.).

6. **Revolving Credit,** credit you can use over and over again (credit cards, personal lines of credit).

7. **Credit Scoring,** uses what is called the **FICO** or the Vantage score, which are the scoring models created to cooperate with the three major credit bureaus known as Experian, Equifax, and TransUnion. Banks, insurance companies, and other types of lenders can have their own types of scoring models.

C. Do You Know How To Fill Out A Credit Application For A Credit Card?

You need to know what to say to lenders to get what you need from them, or what you need to show them. (Not fake check stubs, taxes, or altered bank statements. That will get you locked up. Fraud is real.)

Fill in the Sample Monthly Budget chart below with how much you think your bills will cost per month.

Sample Monthly Budget

Monthly Net Income	
Expense	**Student Estimate**
Rent	
Car Payment	
Food	
Car Insurance	
Gasoline	
Utililties	
Internet	
Cellphone	
Entertainment	
Clothes	
Savings Account	
Total	

This is why you need a bank account. You need to pay your bills from a bank account. It is free to cash your checks with a bank account. It shows people you are responsible and can be trusted when you have a bank account. If you don't have a bank account, it is probably because you can't balance your money, you overspend and have a ton of overdraft fees, or your account is always negative. All those reasons show that your word is bad and that is a red flag, meaning, "Don't trust this person; they may scam you or your bank." The banks will put you in "check systems", letting other banks know your word is not good. This also applies to people who have prepaid cards: They can't be trusted and are probably irresponsible as well.

People who don't make a lot of money need a budget sheet so they can see where they are spending their money. See an example of a Personal Monthly Budget chart on the next page.

7

Why Your Credit Report Matters

Good Credit Report	Bad Credit Report
Saves YOU money	Costs YOU money
Qualify for loans and credit cards	Prevent you from obtaining a loan or credit cards; jeopardize future purchases
Lower interest rate on borrowed money	Prevent you from obtaining a good interest rate
Low cost on car and home insurance	Higher cost on car and home insurance
Obtaining employment	Prevent you from getting a job

 Credit Scores

When you have bills and don't pay them on time every time they are due, it shows people that you aren't trustworthy. You can't balance your money or you would have paid your bills on time because you don't want late fees. Or you aren't making the money you say you make to pay your bills on time. Both of these reasons show you are irresponsible, so who would lend you money? This is one of the most important reasons why lenders won't give you money for a car loan or especially a home loan—your payment record is worthless; nothing matches. If you claim to make a certain amount of money but your lifestyle or your payment history doesn't match, you are lying. Your paperwork will tell everything.

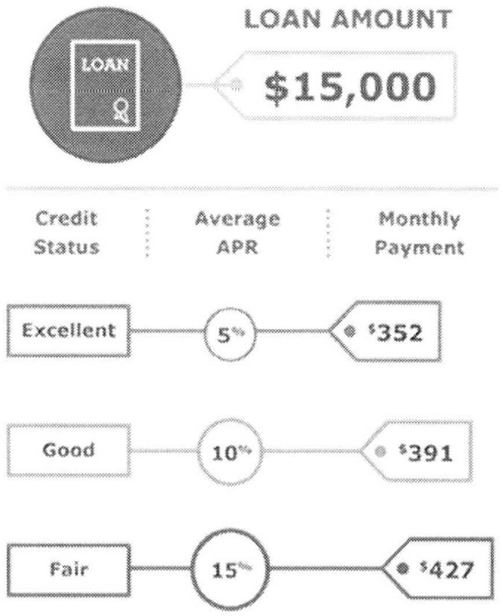

- A **Bad Credit Score** is 579 to 679 and is considered to be high risk. Lenders make you pay more to borrow money.
- A **Good Credit Score** is 680 to 719 and is considered to be low risk. Lenders make you pay less to borrow money. Any score above a 720 is excellent and your rates are lower.
- A **Low Interest Rate** for a car with a 680 or higher credit score is considered good credit (8 to 12%).
- A **High Interest Rate** for a car with a 579 to 679 credit score is considered bad credit (15 to 20%).

Personal Monthly Budget

For the Month of: ______________________

Beginning Month - Checking Account Balance: ____________

1st Paycheck for the Month: ____________

INCOME	Budget	Actual	Difference
Wages & Tips			
PT Income			
Dividends			
Gifts Received			
Refunds/Reimbursements			
Transfer from Savings			
ATM Deposits			
Other			
Total INCOME			

HOME EXPENSES	Budget	Actual	Difference	Due Date	Date Paid
Mortgage/Rent					
Home/Rental Insurance					
Electricity					
Gas/Oil					
Water/Sewer/Trash					
Phone - CELL					
Cable/Satellite					
Alarm					
Furnishings/Appliances					
Lawn/Garden					
Maintenance/Supplies					
Improvements					
Other					
Total HOME EXPENSES					

TRANSPORTATION	Budget	Actual	Difference	Due Date	Date Paid
Vehicle Payments					
Auto Insurance					
Fuel					
Bus/Taxi/Train Fare					
Repairs					
Registration/License					
Other					
Total TRANSPORTATION					

HEALTH	Budget	Actual	Difference	Due Date	Date Paid
Health Insurance (if not taken our of your check					
Doctor/Dentist					
Medicine/Drugs					
Health Club Dues					
Life Insurance					
Veterinarian/Pet Care					
Aflac					
Total HEALTH					

CHARITY/GIFTS	Budget	Actual	Difference	Due Date	Date Paid
Tithing					
Gifts Given					
Charitable Donations					
Other					
Total CHARITY/GIFTS					

SUBSCRIPTIONS	Budget	Actual	Difference	Due Date	Date Paid
Newspaper					
Magazines					
Dues/Memberships					
Other					
Total SUBSCRIPTIONS					

Beginning Month - Savings Account Balance: ____________

DAILY LIVING	Budget	Actual	Difference	Due Date	Date Paid
Groceries					
Personal Supplies					
Clothing					
Cleaning					
Education/Lessons					
Dining/Eating Out					
Salon/Barber					
Pet Food					
PayPal					
Total DAILY LIVING					

ENTERTAINMENT	Budget	Actual	Difference	Due Date	Date Paid
Videos/DVDs					
Music					
Games					
Rentals					
Movies/Theater					
Concerts/Plays					
Books					
Hobbies					
Film/Photos					
Sports					
Outdoor Recreation					
Toys/Gadgets					
Vacation/Travel					
Website					
Total ENTERTAINMENT					

SAVINGS	Budget	Actual	Difference	Due Date	Date Paid
Emergency Fund					
Sinking Fund - 1					
Sinking Fund - 2					
Sinking Fund - 3					
Retirement/Investments					
Other					
Total SAVINGS					

OBLIGATIONS	Budget	Actual	Difference	Due Date	Date Paid
Student Loan					
Other Loan					
Credit Cards - Discover					
Credit Cards - Baraclay					
Federal Taxes					
State/Local Taxes					
Other					
Total OBLIGATIONS					

MISCELLANEOUS	Budget	Actual	Difference	Due Date	Date Paid
Bank Fees					
Postage					
ATM Withdrawls					
Other					
Total MISCELLANEOUS					

BUDGET CATEGORIES

(For creating your own Budget Worksheet)

LIVING / DEBT EXPENSES
Mortgage / Rent
Taxes / HOA
Home / Renter's Insurance
Electricity / Gas/Oil / Water
Sewer / Trash
Cable / Phone / Internet
Cellphone
Tuition
Child Support / Alimony
Childcare
Tutoring / Lessons
Sports / Leagues
Senior Care
Medical / Life / Disability Insurance
Medical Copays / Expenses
Medications
Credit Cards
Personal Loans / Student Loans
Auto Loans & Insurane
Pet Care
Groceries
DISCRETIONARY/ OTHER
Shopping / Clothing
Entertainment / Activities
Subscriptions / Dues
Fitness / Health
Toiletries / Cosmetics / Grooming
Dining Out
Work / School Lunches
Public Parking / Transportation
Gas
Tithing / Charitable Contributions
Bank Fees
Professional Services
Miscellaneous
SAVINGS / INVESTMENTS
Emergency Fund
General Savings
College Savings
IRAs / Retirement
Investments
Second Property Expenses

D. What Do I Need To Buy (Finance) A House?

You will need a job with 2 of your paycheck stubs, 1 to 2 years of your past taxes, down payment money (a percentage of the total cost of purchase), and fair credit to show the lender you are responsible to pay your bills.

E. How And Why Should Kids Need To Build Credit Starting At 14 Years Old?

Once you are of age to get a job, you need to start understanding how money works, how to save half of your check, and how you can apply for a youth credit card or become an authorized user on a family member's credit card to build your credit, but you need to understand how to properly use a credit line. The most important step is to have a small primary credit card for yourself. If you start early, when you get to be 16 years old, you can purchase your own new car.

F. What Is The Best Investment A Person Can Make?

The best investment is to purchase a home or a property; they generally keep their value. You can also use them as collateral and get funding from them. When you purchase an automobile, as soon as you drive off the car lot, it starts to lose value.

There's no point in having a high credit score if you don't know what to do with it. When you go into the bank, let them tell you what they want. Provide what they need and nothing more, so you don't talk yourself out of what you need. People are very judgmental and may think you don't deserve this or that you may not be able to afford it.

G. What Is Bad Debt?

We all have seen people who buy cars and get special accessories to make their cars jump out. What these people don't tell you—or maybe don't know—is that all the extra money they are putting into that car is a waste of money. Once they try to sell the vehicle, they will look at all the money spent on that car and think it is worth so much, but in reality, it depreciates. It looks fun and/or pretty, but has no worth when they try to sell it. They've spent $10,000 on rims, a stereo, hydraulics, motors, suicide doors, custom interiors, but a buyer is not going to carry that cost over. They've trapped themselves into the street cred world that means nothing to a buyer or a financial institution that gives you a true loan-to-value ratio. The **Blue Book Value** is what matters, and if you fill out the information to compute the Blue Book Value, it will only have standardize vehicular information known to the original manufacturer because customized extras cannot be verified.

H. Have You Ever Asked Your Parent(s) What Living Paycheck-To-Paycheck Means?

Most people in America are 1 to 2 paychecks from losing everything. Have you ever thought what would happen if your parents lost their jobs and didn't have any money coming into the home? You understand they could try to get governmental assistance, but that takes a while, so the struggle is real. You will need to learn how to consolidate your debt in order to survive. For example: you may have to sell your car and buy a cheaper car to keep your home, or pawn items at a pawn shop. You may need to get creative to hold on to money so you don't lose everything. You need to talk to a banker to help sort out your finances.

I. Why Do People Rent And Not Own A Home? What's The Difference, And The Pros And Cons?

Renting is flushing your money down the toilet. instead of investing in yourself and building up your own life. Many people rent You are making someone else rich, because they don't know how easy it is to buy a home and live within their means. That means, don't spend money you don't have and put yourself in debt. Remember your word is everything, and if you lose it, no one will believe or work with you.

THE REAL COST OF RENTING

How much will you spend renting in the next year, 5, 10 or 15 years?

If rent is:	1 Year	5 Years	10 Years	15 Years
$500	$6,000	$30,000	$60,000	$90,000
$600	$7,200	$36,000	$72,000	$108,000
$700	$8,400	$42,000	$84,000	$126,000
$800	$9,600	$48,000	$96,000	$144,000
$900	$10,800	$54,000	$108,000	$162,000
$1,000	$12,000	$60,000	$120,000	$180,000
$1,100	$13,200	$66,000	$132,000	$198,000
$1,200	$14,400	$72,000	$144,000	$216,000
$1,300	$15,600	$78,000	$156,000	$234,000
$1,400	$16,800	$84,000	$168,000	$252,000
$1,500	$18,000	$90,000	$180,000	$270,000
$1,600	$19,200	$96,000	$192,000	$288,000

Wouldn't you rather put that money into your own home and build equity in an investment?

STEPS TO PURCHASING A HOUSE

	Notes
How Much House Can You Afford?	
Know Your Debt-to-Income Ratio	
Be Aware of All 3 Credit Scores (Equifax, TransUnion, Experian)	
Contact a Loan Officer	
Shop For a Loan	
Contact a Realtor	
Learn About Home Buying Programs	
Have a Minimum of 10% For a Down Payment	
Have a Stable Employment History	
Be Able to Provide at Least 3 to 6 Paystubs	
Provide Bank and Tax Statements	
Shop For a Home	
Make an Offer	
Get and Pay For a Home Inspection	
Shop For Home Owners Insurance	
Sign Papers	
Pay Closing Costs	
Moving Costs	
Things to Consider When Looking for a House	
Location: City, Suburbs, Golf Course, Gated Community, Waterfront	
Style: Bungalow, Colonial, Ranch	
Home Types: Single Family, Attached/Detached, Condo, Townhome, Manufactured	
Room Types: Bedroom, Bathrooms, Basement, Living Space	
Flooring: Carpeting, Wood, Concrete, Tile, Laminate	
Kitchen Features: Built-in/Freestanding Stainless, Cabinetry; Islands/Wet Bars	
Bath Features: Dual/Triple Sinks, Separate Shower, Jetted/Sunken Tubs, Vanities	

J. Why Do My Decisions Make A Difference?

When you are growing up, every choice you make will affect your future, especially when you break the law. Decisions may seem simple and/or irrelevant because you don't always get caught, but once you get older, you will have a hard time getting a job and surviving. It's called consequences and repercussions. If you know how to do things the right way, you don't have to worry, but people often are not taught the right way. There are four rules in life you can follow to not have trouble:

1. No Stealing.
2. No Drugs.
3. No Bad and Illegal Intent.
4. No violence.

K. What's The Difference Between Store Cards And Other Credit Cards?

Credit cards are considered primary cards that boost your credit if you make sure you pay your limits down as explained above. A store credit card is also great. It can help you build your credit as well, but you can only use it at the store that issued it. You need both types of cards to build you credit properly.

L. Why Is It Important To Do Things The Right Way Vs. Doing Things The Wrong Way?

Short cuts can be easy but aren't always right. Many people don't pay their taxes to the government and get into a lot of trouble because they are scared and may not understand. They don't have to avoid paying taxes. The government will give you a payment plan, so why are you scared?

There is a right way and a wrong way to do things. Usually, if you get caught doing something the wrong way, the consequences are far higher (worse) than if you had done it the right way from the start.

M. Can I Turn My Life And My Credit Around?

People try to take the easy way out by filling bankruptcy, but they may just need a good credit repair. Check out places like *stickysituations.info.* They can help you fix your credit, get a loan, understand how money works, and quickly boost your credit.

N. What Is The Difference Between An Employee And An Entrepreneur?

Employees work for others. They do what they are told, they don't take risks, and often specialize in a role to get paid for their services. They play it safe because they know life would be too difficult to survive without the security of a job, and they are use to a nine-to-five work schedule.

Entrepreneurs live for the risk. They listen, and they have to be very savvy because if they don't make money, they don't eat. Entrepreneurs get paid for results. They generally work around the clock. They never know when they'll need to have a meeting, and they work extremely long hours. They are always putting out fires. They believe enough in themselves to make it happen for them.

O. What Is A Realistic Job And Salary?

Skilled Trade Jobs and Salaries

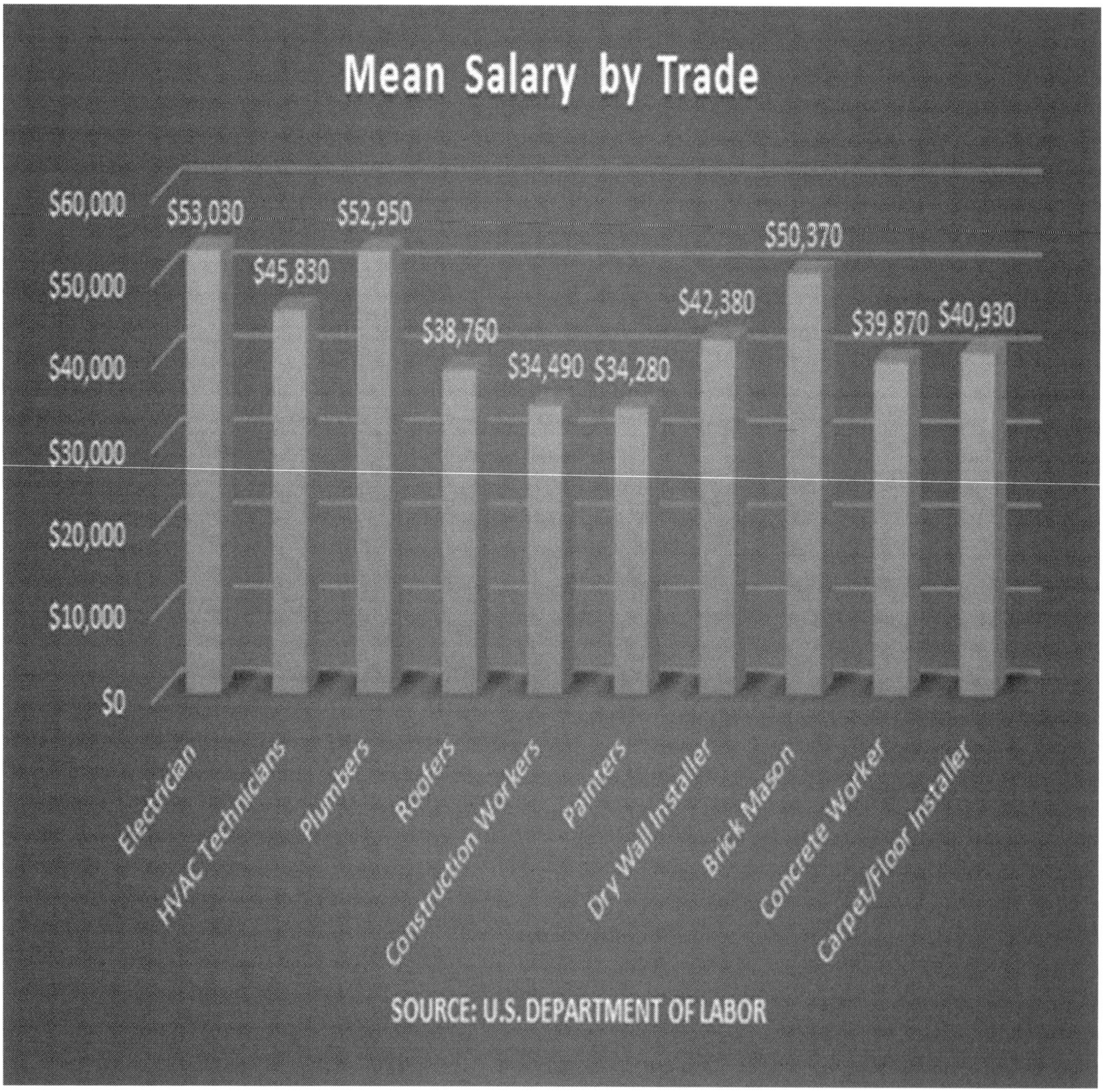

BY KRYSTAL BANKS

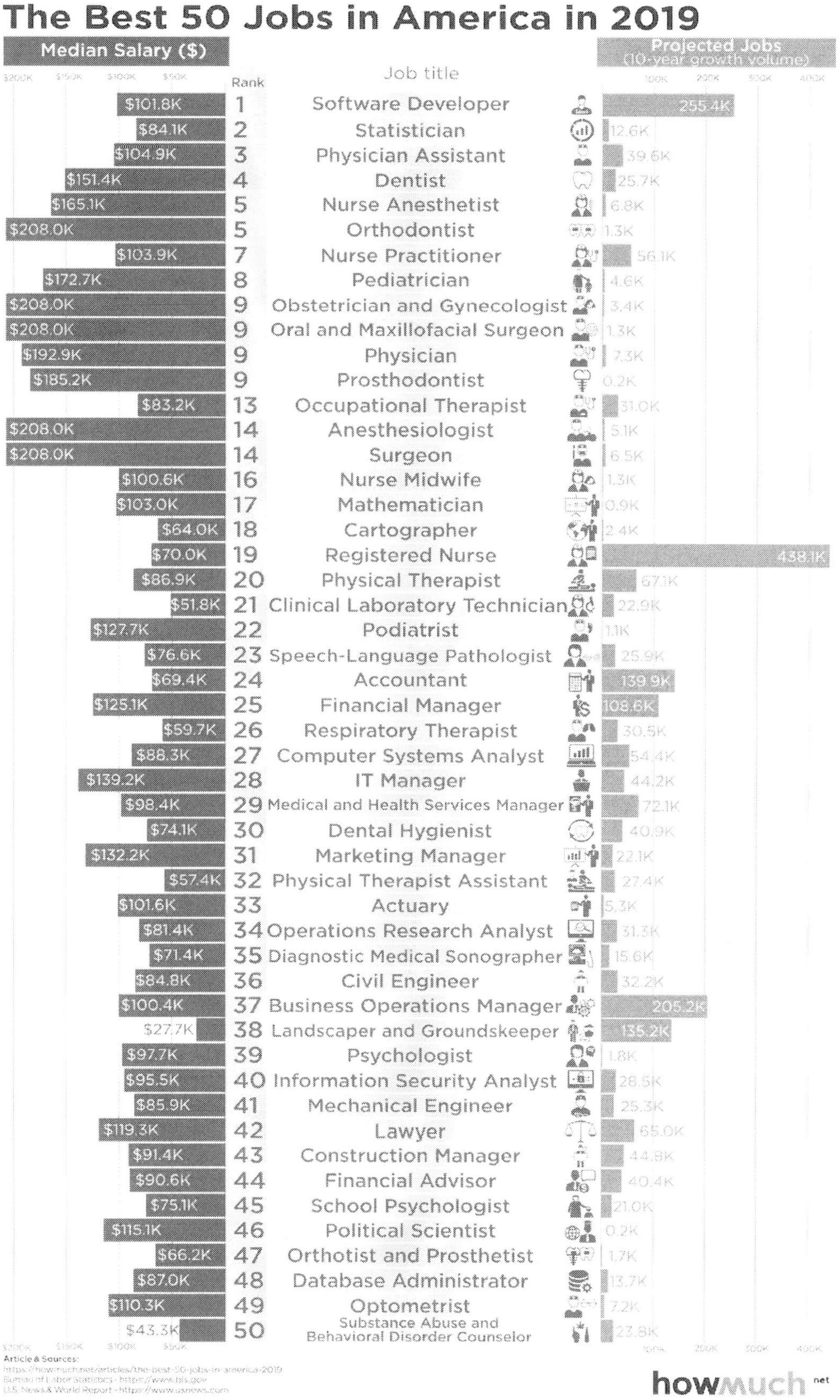

Price of College Per Year

8. Economics And How It Relates To You

People often talk about how rich people make all their money off the poor. It's called understanding economics and it's true, but it's up to you to change that. Understanding how powerful your dollar in your community is, is the beginning. Knowing the things you need the most to survive and where to spend your money is the solution. For example: Most people drive used cars. So, what does that mean to you? It means that somewhere in your neighborhood is some type of auto parts store and mechanic shops because used cars are more likely to break down and need parts and repairs, and they are going to overcharge you. This is why you do your research and get three quotes before getting repairs; it's worth the savings.

This applies to discounted stores like Dollar General or the small liquor store as well. These are popular stores where the average person spends a lot of money daily or weekly over a period of time. In these types of stores, often they are higher priced because of convenience, but many of these stores sell people outdated products because people don't pay attention to the dates of the items or they get them at a discounted rate. It is illegal to sell outdated items. You must get a receipt, take pictures, then report the spoiled item to the proper authorities, like the USDA and the attorney general.

I'm explaining this because when you go to rural areas, like in the country, they do not have these same types of stores surrounding their neighborhoods, specifically increasing their community dollar value. This is why it is so important to travel and get out of your local area, so you can see how differently the rest of the world operates. Outside your community, other areas typically don't have a liquor store on every corner to keep you mentally impaired. This is called targeting audiences in certain demographics. Another example of that is when you watch local television and you see a lot of commercials encouraging you to purchase junk that is irrelevant to your life (marketing). So, if you want to save money, you need to spend it on items that are necessities to you. The marketing strategy is all about area and timing. This is why around dinner time you see a lot of commercials for food—to entice you to go to a fast-food restaurant. Notice they only promote the specials like 5-for-$5, but when you order one value meal, it's now $8. Those fast-food restaurants spend a lot of money because they are close to your area and so YOU will spend your money. Every dollar counts.

Notice if you're in the country that you hardly see any fast-food restaurants, so when you do go into town, you are spending your money wisely. You are probably asking yourself, "What does this have to do with being rich or poor?" Well, generally, when you are poor, you get some type of food assistance. The issue is the price you pay for processed food versus what the food assistance program was actually meant for: to buy food to cook that will last longer while being on a budget. Go to your local store and price out these products to stay under $30 for 5 days.

Branding
(Name Brand vs. Non-Name Brand)

Local Store Price	Item	Kroger/ Meijer Price	No. of Servings
$ ________	Hot Pockets	$ ________	______
$ ________	Pizza Rolls	$ ________	______
$ ________	Taquitos	$ ________	______
$ ________	Chicken Nuggets	$ ________	______
$ ________	Fruit Snacks	$ ________	______
$ ________	Frozen French Fries	$ ________	______
$ ________	Ground Beef	$ ________	______
$ ________	Spaghetti Noodles	$ ________	______
$ ________	Spaghetti Sauce	$ ________	______
$ ________	Pack of Chicken	$ ________	______
$ ________	Bag of Rice	$ ________	______
$ ________	Frozen Vegetables	$ ________	______
$ ________	Sack of Potatoes	$ ________	______
$ ________	Bread	$ ________	______
$ ________	Gallon of Milk	$ ________	______
$ ________	Cooking Oil	$ ________	______

Seeing how you waste money should teach you to pay attention to economics—how the world works!—because you don't know what you've never been taught. When you are shopping, you need to understand couponing and getting discounts. You get more bang for your buck if it costs you less, and you'll have more money to spend on something else.

The same concepts apply on a larger scale and the scale starts out with what is important to you—your priorities. Let's make a chart, writing down your priorities, starting with the most-important goals you want to achieve. (*See the example.*) Remember the difference between a goal and a wish: A goal is written down with a step-by-step timeline to get you to finish by a deadline. A wish is what you want, but there's rarely any direction to get it. That's why so many wishes don't come true.

Priority Chart

Sample Priority List

1. Get a job ($20 per hour) and/or training/education.
2. Get a bank account (learning to budget).
3. Build credit/get a credit card (not overspending).
4. Save money/small investment.
5. Buy first home.
6. Buy a car (maybe an upgraded car).
7. Travel/partying.
8. Start a family.
9. Stay fresh (new clothes).

Your Priority List *(please list in order of importance)*

1. ______________________________
2. ______________________________
3. ______________________________
4. ______________________________
5. ______________________________
6. ______________________________
7. ______________________________
8. ______________________________
9. ______________________________
10. ______________________________

The reason the order is most important is because if you follow the sample chart, chances are your life will work out easier and you can accomplish your goals faster. You can go out of order, but it may be harder to achieve your goal if, for example, you have a child before you achieve the other goals. They are expensive, making it harder for you to focus on your priorities.

Now that you have a focus on your future, you need to see how the economy and politics directly affect your life. People generally think they understand buying, selling, trading, and gambling, but do they really? The answer is NO, because if they did, they would be more responsible with their money, getting to move on up to the next level. Stop being ***BROKE***! On most news channels, you constantly see the NASDAQ, DOW, S&P, but do you ever wonder what they are talking about and how it relates to you?

An investment is the purchase of assets that are not consumed today but are used to create future wealth. The goal is to increase the value of the assets above the purchase price to achieve a profit or an income over time. For example, if you paid $2500 and the assets increased to $3500, your profit is $1000. There are 4 types of assets or investments:

- Stock: ownership share of a company.
- Bonds: lender of funds to a company or government that pays interest income.
- Real estate: landlord of housing, retail, office, or industrial space.
- Collectibles: art, antique cars, jewelry, watches, or wine.

The most-discussed asset/investment is stock, as its price is disclosed to the public on stock exchanges, known as the stock market. Stock prices go up and down 5 days a week as traders buy and sell on the behalf of individuals and funds on the stock exchanges. There are 3 major stock exchanges in the U.S., where all prices are disclosed to the public:

- NYSE: New York Stock Exchange
- AMEX: American Stock Exchange, where traders buy and sell stock on a trading floor
- NASDAQ: National Association of Securities Dealers Automated Quotations System, where stock is bought and sold through an automated system

There are 3 indexes that measure the performance of stock listed on the US stock exchanges. These indexes are:

- Dow Jones Industrial Average: measures 30 top industrial stocks listed on stock exchanges
- S&P 500: measures 500 large companies listed on stock exchanges in the United States
- NASDAQ: measures newer startup companies listed on the NASDAQ stock market

Sometimes the profit comes over a longer period of time or in a short time, but the formula

(Selling Price per share x Number of shares) – (Purchase Price per share x Number of shares) = PROFIT

Here is an example of generating a fortune over 10 years. Dollar General, listed with the symbol DG, had an Initial Price Offering (IPO) at $21 per share on 11/17/2009. As of 4/17/2020, your shares were valued at $183 per share, for a profit $162 per share. If you owned 1000 shares, your profit would be $162,000.

(Selling Price per share x Number of shares) – (Purchase Price per share x Number of shares) = PROFIT
($183 per share x 1000) – ($21 per shares x 1000) = PROFIT
($183,000) – ($21,000) = ***$162,000***

Even during the COVID -19 coronavirus crisis, people were making short-term profits. Here is an example: Zoom Communications, listed with the symbol ZM, had an Initial Price Offering (IPO) at $36 per share on 4/17/2019. As of 4/17/2020, your shares were valued at $150 per share, for a profit $114 per share.

(Selling Price per share x Number of shares) – (Purchase Price per share x Number of shares) = PROFIT
($150 per share x 1000) – ($36 per shares x 1000) = PROFIT
($150,000) – ($36,000) = ***$114,000***

If you had sold Zoom when it achieved its highest price of $164.94, your profit would be $128.94 per share.

Some stocks deliver a steady price year in and year out. Others are driven by events and circumstance.

Choose a few companies you admire. Look up their Initial Public Offering (IPO) price which is the purchase price for this equation and then their price as of today which is the selling price.

- Company: ______________________________
- Stock Symbol: ______________________________
- IPO Date: ______________________________

(Selling Price per share x Number of shares) – (Purchase Price per share x Number of shares) = PROFIT

($______ per share x 1000) – ($______ per shares x 1000) = PROFIT

($__________) – ($__________) = $__________

- Company: ______________________________
- Stock Symbol: ______________________________
- IPO Date: ______________________________

(Selling Price per share x Number of shares) – (Purchase Price per share x Number of shares) = PROFIT

($______ per share x 1000) – ($______ per shares x 1000) = PROFIT

($__________) – ($__________) = $__________

- Company: ______________________________
- Stock Symbol: ______________________________
- IPO Date: ______________________________

(Selling Price per share x Number of shares) – (Purchase Price per share x Number of shares) = PROFIT

($______ per share x 1000) – ($______ per shares x 1000) = PROFIT

($__________) – ($__________) = $__________

Often companies that cater to the middle/lower class and the mass market do well. The volume of people they are servicing makes them valuable. So do companies whose services are in high demand. Your job is to follow trends, which requires researching general and financial news every day to "BET" on the companies that will do well. Often, it is the companies you use in your daily life. Knowing this type of information:

- Paying attention to current events
- Understanding what is happening with the top financial companies and how it will trickle down to your life
- And, if you can follow how their money works

will teach you how to invest and change where your money goes. When you see and understand money, you generally don't have to break the law. Most people break the law because they are looking for a quick buck.

In school, you have a student council that imitates how the government works, but do you understand how it relates to you personally? When you are in school and can't get through to a staff member, the student union is supposed to listen to your problem and work on a negotiation to resolve your issue. If you can't get a resolution there, you may have to go to a counselor, dean, or assistant principal. That is called following the proper chain of command or protocol. You need to know this information because the same rules apply in life. The difference in life is, as an adult, you have the right to vote, and the power to vote means you can control the people who make the rules. Understanding how money works at the top will show you the changes on your life. When the Big 3 fell, it almost sent a lot of people into a depression.

A. Conflict Resolution

No matter who you are or where you are from, conflict is inevitable and recurring. Often, people look at conflict as something bad, but without conflict, there will never be change and resolve. That is what business and life is all about. You have a problem and how you deal with it can result in a positive or negative change. You are trying to get the result you want out of the situation, but often you being angry, having an attitude, or being disrespectful tends to change the mood of the situation, making your situation worse. Now imagine, instead of being rude or nasty with another person:

1. You explore some critical-thinking skills, the art of negotiation, looking at it from their point of view.

2. You speak to them in a nice, positive manner.

3. You are willing to meet them half way.

Oftentimes, the greater problem is not the conflict, but the inability to navigate through these challenging sticky situations. Explore topics such as self-awareness, external triggers, and strategies to navigate and manage conflict.

So often, many people find themselves in minor situations that escalate into major altercations because they failed to take the necessary steps to resolve the conflict. The truth is, most of us were never taught how to de-escalate and navigate through conflict. Our natural response is to yell at the person who is yelling at us. If your goal is to be extremely frustrated or to just argue non-stop, then congratulations. Without the necessary tools and understanding, you will more than likely go in circles without any resolution to your problems. You will drive your blood pressure up and cause unnecessary anxiety while making no forward progress in resolving your conflict. However, if you are looking to better yourself and change the outcome of some of the bad situations in your life, you will need to learn how to effectively resolve conflict.

We all need help sometimes. This is no different with conflict resolution. If you are not able to resolve conflict one-on-one, do not hesitate to find a person or party who might be able to mediate your situation. This can be done with a professional mediator or just an unbiased third party. Resolving conflict is not always easy, but it is possible. When we have situations we need to resolve, there are some things we need to keep in mind. When resolving conflict, we should:

1. Attempt to stay calm.
2. Regulate our own emotions.
3. Listen to those who have conflict with us.
4. Communicate effectively. (Talk it out.)
5. Be prepared to compromise if necessary.
6. Most importantly, LISTEN to what is being said.

***

9. *Working Budget Vs. Non-Working Budget*

We need to do a comparison on how being on welfare directs our lives. If you or your family have never had a job and have only collected welfare/Section 8, you generally don't understand how to make money work for yourself. If you did, you would use the Section 8 income to buy a home. They do have programs to do this, but you probably have never heard of it. Many people don't understand how far money goes when you work hard for a living. When you go to work every day, you spend approximately 8 hours a day, totaling 40 hours a week, making money and generally not spending money. You then sleep approximately 7 hours a day, totaling 49 hours a week. This leaves you with 87 hours a week of idle time. So, if you are not working, you may be spending money, and spending money you do not have.

If you work, you generally are paid an hourly wage. You should know how much your monthly bills are, create a budget, and stay within that budget to be able to afford your means of living. You may be able to pick up extra hours to make extra money so you can save or purchase something, especially if you have some unexpected expense that occurs. These people tend to be more reserved in their spending because they have laid out a plan and have to follow it to get what they want. Now let's compare this to, say a person who is completely dependent on a welfare system or just in poverty. They bring in under $19,000 a year; that's minimum wage for a year. They possibly are getting Section 8 for housing, so they do not have to pay a lot of money for rent, just a percentage—maybe $100 or less a month. They get discounts on utilities and better payment arrangements on the bills. Then, there is food. They get a monthly stipend to purchase non-processed foods to stretch their money for their family. So, what gives these people any incentive to get off welfare? Some people will get off because they understand it is a temporary situation, while others won't get off until they are kicked off; then, their lives get worse. What would give you the inspiration to get a job to take care of your family? Possibly buying a home of your own or a car?

While you are on assistance, you can start your own business and collect the freebies until you build your worth. Also, your kids can go to college free! Something in you must say, "How do I make a plan to get out of this situation and possibly move into a better home, one that I can call my own, one that is an investment for my future?" Have you ever asked the question, "Who pays for these people to be able to live on a lower budget?" Well, people who are working get a percentage taken from their checks that's called taxes. In the event they fall on hard times and lose their jobs, the government can subsidize them until they get another job and get back on their feet. The key word is subsidize; that means it is a substitute, meaning not permanent. But often people believe they don't have to work and can live off this system. Many people think this is just free money, but it comes with a price. You will generally ALWAYS be BROKE! It is up to you to get a well-paying job, trade, and/or education so you can make better money to not be in this system.

This system is building a debt for the future generations. In today's time, we are currently under a trillion-dollar deficit. That means, for the next 50-100 years, our kids are going to have to find a way to pay for this huge debt we are in.

A. Future Planning Case Studies

Case Study 1: You have people out here who take advantage of the welfare system and that's the problem, Generational Welfare. Perhaps everyone in their family has always been on assistance. No one works—not parents, aunts and uncles, or grandparents—I mean no one, and they are only taught to continue getting assistance. We all know those people who, let's say, are on assistance and perhaps live in a family home. They don't work and they take care of a family member who gets a check for some type of disability. They also have different sources of income like social security, maybe a few kids they get a check for, and they are milking the system. The problem with this situation is they may have a good income, but they tend to never be able to better themselves or their kids' lives. They still live in poverty and they can't—or perhaps don't want to—work hard to move to the next level. They may not consider where they live to be the hood or an urban area, because they have never been anywhere else to compare it to.

We first have to establish what is considered the hood. Is it safe in your neighborhood? Or, are you constantly in danger or worried about your home being broken into? Do you have bars on your doors and windows? Glass block in your windows? If you go 5 miles surrounding your home, does your property value decrease? Urban areas generally have more check cashing stores than banks. Can you go into a store but can't go to the bathroom? If you can't go on vacations for a week without worrying that someone is going to break into your home, you may not be in a safe area. And when there are safety issues, eventually the government may take over the neighborhood and do what is called gentrification; that's a hostile takeover. They tear down the whole neighborhood and rebuild, but this time when they rebuild, most of the people who lived in the neighborhood will not be able to afford the homes, raising the cost of living.

How would you change and get out of this generational situation?

____

____

____

____

____

____

____

Case Study 2: Lisa is married with four kids and lives in a house she inherited from her parents, meaning she does not have to pay a mortgage. All she has to do is keep up with the taxes, pay utilities, and house maintenance. One of the four children is chronically ill and she collects social security benefits for this child of $900 a month. Lisa does not work but is a caregiver for her child, receiving $1000 monthly for caregiving. Lisa's husband has a factory job making $20,800 a year, that's $10 per hour. He lives in the home (but not on the record) and pays child support, only bringing home $200 a week. Jenny is a friend who is living with Lisa. She has 5 kids, 2 of which collect social security benefits in the amount of $1200 a month. Between the 3 adults and 8 kids, they receive $1100 a month in food assistance. What is their total monthly income?

B. Standards

Do you have a standard in life? What are acceptable standards to you?

1. ____
2. ____
3. ____
4. ____
5. ____

What are you supposed to know in life? You are supposed to know how to read, write, do math, and have an understanding of societal skills. But you are also supposed to know about working and surviving; how and why you need a job; what to research to help your situation; and, how money works.

What is surviving to you? Do you have the standard skills to survive? What does it take to get ahead in life? Let's talk about roles and responsibilities. Whose job is it to teach you how to be a productive citizen, your parents or your teachers? What happens if they fail?

C. Understanding The Gray Areas Of Life

1. Who sets your standards?
   a. Yourself
   b. Your parents
   c. Teachers
   d. Social media
   e. Relationship with a higher being
2. What do you view as a good standard? (For example: having a job, money, a stable family, a new car, a house, new clothes, or being on welfare)
   a. ______________________________
   b. ______________________________
   c. ______________________________
   d. ______________________________
   e. ______________________________
3. Who do you value and why do you value them?

   ____
   ____
   ____
   ____
   ____
4. What are you willing to do to get to your standards?

   ____
   ____
   ____
   ____
   ____
5. How do you get to your standards?

   ____
   ____
   ____
   ____
   ____

6. Give me an example of compromising your standards? (For example, spending too much money on vacation or Christmas but falling behind on you bills)

____

____

____

____

____

D. Looking Rich Vs. Being Rich

Most people will spend their money on useless items. If you can't balance $100, you can balance $1,000,000. Understanding money is the difference between looking rich versus being rich. If you can't pay your bills on time with small bills, you won't be able to pay your bills when you get more money and more bills. This is the reason many celebrities go broke. They don't know how to budget and invest. They spend so much money on things that are irrelevant to show off that the debt eats them alive.

E. The Ugly Conversation About Racism

1. Respect, Listen, and Awareness

People understand that everyone is not going to get along with each other. You may go to school or work with different types of people, or maybe you go to school or work with the same type of people as yourself. Knowing and recognizing the differences with people should only make you focus on one thing: Respect. In our current times, people often forget about always showing others the respect you want them to give you. Respect is a two-way street; you have to give it to get it. Unfortunately, everyone doesn't play by these same rules. As you go through life, there are many people who cannot control themselves and, therefore, show a nasty attitude. By having a bad attitude, you can change the situation, making life harder than it should be.

Everyone knows someone who is sarcastic and people don't generally take them seriously because of their smart mouth, and people tend to read them wrong. This can come across as conflict, which is a lack of communicating with others in a respectable way. In life, we will find ourselves going through different situations based off many differences. There is a saying: You get more with honey than you do vinegar. That means, if you are nice to people, they will listen and you probably will get your way, versus if you are mean or rude to people, they will make it hard for you to get what you want.

People may not like you because you are different from them. That could mean race, color, or creed. Whatever it is, they could find a reason to dislike you and you could find a reason to dislike them. Does that mean you are supposed to be rude or disrespectful? NO! That will never make the situation better. As you grow up, you will have to address people—perhaps your teachers or coworkers, maybe even your bosses—and maybe you won't like them for various reasons. It is up to you to take the high road and remain nice and professional to everyone. Many times, you may not recognize racism or jealousy, but it definitely does exist. If someone favors you more than them, people treat you better than others, or even if they are embarrassed that they don't know what you know and perhaps you may pass them by in life, you must always remain respectful and not take it to heart. It is your job to remain humble and understand what and why that person may be going through what they are going through. Put yourself in their shoes.

Do you know what nepotism or cronyism is? That's when people have forms of favoritism by being a relative or a friend. For example, someone only got the job because of their cousin or best friend's kid. You know they will get treated better than you. They may get raises they don't deserve, or people believe them over you because of their connection(s). It happens in the world more than you know; connections are real. You need to be aware of the situation so you can make the right decision.

Some issues people often have with racism is they can't relate to other people, so it often needs to be broken down to others. Like, how would you feel if this happened to you? Then discuss what would you do to open the conversation up.

***

10. Human/Sex Trafficking

I never hear parents say, "My good child can get a bad sentence." They say they prepare their kids, but do they? Do you, as a minor, know how dangerous it is out here for you? Your parents may be scared to tell you the truth, but I want you to understand how serious it is for you to pay attention to people and your surroundings. People are snatching children, and drugging and selling them as sex slaves and for body parts. I don't think young people realize how horrifying that situation is!

You need to recognize the signs of human trafficking. Simple things like: no eye contact with the people around them; signs of abuse—black eyes, bruises, etc.; wearing sexually-provocative clothing; dating older people; having no I.D.; can't explain where their money is coming from; people who control them who won't let them speak for themselves. If you see any of these signs—***OR YOU ARE GOING THROUGH THIS***—you'd better tell as many people as you can as soon as you can. Don't be ashamed to tell someone you got caught up in something you weren't prepared for and you need help to get out of it. Leave signs or just run! It could be the difference between life and death.

You may be walking every day by a house where people are being held against their will. It is a dangerous world out here and no one talks to minors about crimes. You have to be aware of your surroundings at all times to avoid bad situations—or, so you can get away from them. You should always keep in touch with your parents or someone to let them know where you are and what you're doing. You never know who might be watching you, preparing to take you. If you have regular habits and you're dependable about checking in, if something unfortunate were to happen to you, the sooner someone recognizes that something isn't right, the better!

A VERY SERIOUS ISSUE TODAY IS SOCIAL MEDIA. Young people today have an ***IT-WON'T-HAPPEN-TO-ME*** mentality. The truth is, when you meet new people on social media platforms, a lot of times you don't really know to whom you are talking. You see, like, then friend someone because something on their profile looks good to you, never thinking that could be a fake profile to lure you in. You don't really know them. Or, they say something funny and now you're their friend. ***WAKE UP! HACKING PROFILES IS REAL!*** Predators use fake images to lure young girls ***AND BOYS*** into meeting them, so they can kidnap, drug, rape, and/or sell them into sexual slavery.

Here are 11 facts about human trafficking from DoSomething.org.

1. Globally, the average cost of a slave is $90. (A ***PERSON*** is bought for less than $100.)

2. Trafficking primarily involves exploitation, which comes in many forms, including: forcing victims into prostitution, subjecting victims to slavery or involuntary servitude, and compelling victims to commit sex acts to create pornography. Even though you may say it was your choice to have sex, especially with several people, it still is a crime when you're a minor. You think you know what you're doing or want, but you don't; not yet. Not to mention, most times, you aren't thinking of the possible long-term consequences.

3. According to some estimates, approximately 80% of trafficking involves sexual exploitation, and 19% involves labor exploitation. (They get paid off your hard work and you get ***NOTHING!***)

4. ***THERE ARE APPROXIMATELY 20 TO 30 MILLION SLAVES IN THE WORLD TODAY.***

5. According to the U.S. State Department, 600,000 to 800,000 people are trafficked across international borders every year, of which 80% are female and half are children. That means, ***1 OUT OF EVERY 5*** victims is male. (Guys, these old perverts and cougars want you!)

6. ***THE AVERAGE AGE A TEEN ENTERS THE SEX TRADE IN THE U.S. IS 12-TO-14 YEARS OLD. MANY VICTIMS ARE RUNAWAY GIRLS WHO WERE SEXUALLY ABUSED AS CHILDREN.*** *(Don't think people you know won't set you up for a quick dollar!)*

7. California harbors 3 of the FBI's 13 highest child sex trafficking areas in the nation: Los Angeles, San Francisco, and San Diego. (***BEWARE:*** This is not just a "big city"

problem! This is happening everywhere, even in your small town! They just don't talk about it or tell you about it!)

8. The National Human Trafficking Hotline receives more calls from Texas than any other state in the US. 15% of those calls are from the Dallas-Fort Worth area.

9. ***Between 14,500 and 17,500 people are trafficked into the U.S. each year.***

10. Human trafficking is the third largest international crime industry (behind illegal drugs and arms trafficking). It reportedly generates a profit of $32 billion every year. Of that number, $15.5 billion is made in industrialized countries. (*These are heartless people getting rich—or getting richer!)*

11. The International Labour Organization estimates that women and girls represent the largest share of forced labor victims with 11.4 million trafficked victims (55%) compared to 9.5 million (45%) men. *(I hope you're paying attention to these numbers. It could be you!)*

If you believe you are the victim of a trafficking situation or may have information about a potential trafficking situation, call the National Human Trafficking Resource Center (NHTRC) at 1-888-373-7888. NHTRC is a national, toll-free hotline, with specialists available to answer calls from anywhere in the country, 24 hours a day, seven days a week, every day of the year related to potential trafficking victims, suspicious behaviors, and/or locations where trafficking is suspected to occur.

A. A Message To Youths From Someone Who Works On An Internet Crimes Against Children (ICAC) Task Force

In today's generation, technology plays a huge role in most people's everyday lives. I remember when we had beepers and cellphones that looked like huge blocks and were probably just as heavy. Over 90% of U.S. households have more than one electronic device according to recent research. Today's youths are use to electronic devices. By the age of three, most of them can use any device you place in front of them better than most adults. It is important that children are taught how to practice safety on the Internet. Monitoring and the use of parental controls are also paramount in this era. The reasons are many, but more so, if not done, the consequences can be serious and *even deadly*.

Our youths have access to the Internet at almost every turn. Let's face it, taking electronics away is a great consequence and punishment for bad behavior, but they still will be able to gain access when they are at school or with friends who have devices. The Internet is used for many reasons and the reasons continue to grow; therefore, technology will only continue to grow. Most kids under the age of 18 have no idea what an encyclopedia is, but they sure know what *Wikipedia* is. More and more people are reading books on tablets or other devices. There are as many pros as there are cons regarding technology.

As I work in this field on a daily basis, I see the ages of the children getting younger and younger regarding those being exposed to inappropriate material on the Internet. Furthermore, I see live victims who are extremely young being exploited online, some still in diapers. I have seen more child-on-child sex crimes in the last few years than I have in my entire 18-year career thus far. When speaking to these children, they usually disclose they saw something on television or the Internet that was sexual in nature, thus making them "curious". So how is this happening without the parents or guardians knowing? I believe the answer is awareness and education. The days of households with two parents and only one working is a thing of the past. Most households have either two working parents or one single parent or guardian who works. When a parent or guardian is absent from the home, children will get on social media and the Internet if they have access to any type of devices to occupy them or babysit them.

Let us not forget the massive amounts of peer pressure and cyber bullying that occur online. Today's youths face a completely different type of peer pressure and bullying than the generation prior to them. The anonymity of the Internet allows pedophiles and predators to prey on children using many disguises. More and more kids are taking naked selfies and sending them to other kids requesting them. Some are sending them to others they believe to be kids, but in actuality, are adults posing as children to exploit that child. As sick as it is, child pornography in a multi-billion-dollar industry. Once they send that image, it's out there forever. Children or adolescents who are sending and exchanging pictures or video with their boyfriends or girlfriends which are sexual in nature usually have an argument or break up. At that point, those images and video are posted on social media and sent to all their friends and even family at times. Our youths would describe this as *going viral*. They do not realize they are manufacturing, possessing, then distributing child pornography. These are serious crimes that carry serious penalties.

However, as we know, there must be intent to charge someone with a crime. This means our youths must also be educated regarding these laws. There also seems to be this growing trend regarding how many followers a child has on social media websites. They are accepting people into their social circle they've never met or even heard of. When they think they're speaking to 16-year-old Bobby, it may really be a 45-year-old sexual predator named Bobby. Communicating and instant messaging a person the youth has never seen or met is seen far too often nowadays. This is truly a recipe for disaster. Children and adolescents are meeting up with adult individuals and engaging in sex acts without a parent or guardian ever finding out until it's too late. I've seen many real child victims in my career and I have saved many children from being victimized by going online in an undercover capacity. It would be easy to discuss every single case I've worked, but what I feel is more important is to discuss the ramifications of what can occur when a child or adolescent is not safe online and to also bring awareness regarding the dangers when a child doesn't use safe practices while online.

I recall the very moment I learned that such awful things happened to our youth online. In fact, I will share the story that motivated me to pursue this field with all my heart. I had the opportunity to meet this victim in person and listen to her story. In 2002, Alecia Kozakiewicz, a beautiful 13-year-old girl, was taken from outside her home and held in a dungeon-type basement for several days after meeting up with someone she had been chatting with in a Yahoo chatroom for several months. Chatrooms were immensely popular back then and have kind of phased out; however, there are many that still exist. But other applications and social media have taken over in a more intrusive manner. Nevertheless, on that very cold January night in Pittsburg, Alicia had no idea she would be meeting a 38-year-old man, as she believed she was communicating with someone completely different.

When she stepped outside her house to meet her new friend from the Yahoo chatroom, she was taken and brought to a home where she was held hostage, sexually assaulted, and tortured for almost 4 days. She was chained to the floor with nothing but a leather collar around her neck. This was a white female who had a good life. She had a nice home and loving parents. She was not abused or a "problem child". Her parents had no idea what she was doing online—not because they didn't care, they just weren't aware that such things were happening on the Internet. They had no idea what chatrooms even were.

Alicia was your "average" 13-year-old girl. During those four days this child was abducted by this predator, she waited and waited for help. This child was abused, weak, and tired, but she prayed for the first time in her life. In law enforcement, finding this child after four days would almost seem impossible; however, in this case, Alicia was lucky and rescued by the FBI ICAC Task Force. Although this occurred in Pittsburgh, a huge break in the case came from a Florida man who made a tip regarding a video he had seen online. This 38-year-old predator had videotaped her and posted the video online while bragging about what he had done.

Following Alicia's rescue, she began to share her story all the way into her adulthood. Her story is very public and powerful. It became Alicia's mission in life to help as many kids as possible to NOT become victims. This story plays out every single day, yet most refuse to understand that this type of evil truly exists, especially our youths!

Too many children are becoming addicted to pornography because they're surfing the web all night instead of going to sleep. This then makes them tired at school, but more so, can make them act out sexually with other children. The safety of children and adolescents on the Internet is not something one person or one parent can fix. It's truly a joint effort for everyone to do their part, including the youths. The more awareness these children have at an early age, the better decisions they can make when confronted with these issues. People are not just born with critical-thinking skills. Critical thinking is the objective analysis of facts to form a judgment. This is a valuable life skill. Learning refusal skills and how to say no is super important and should be taught in the home. By practicing refusal skills, it will teach youths how to critically think.

Parents and youths should know who the sex offenders and predators are in your area and where they reside. Parent should know where their children are, as there are many ways to track their location if they have an electronic device. Children and adolescents need to ensure an adult knows their whereabouts at all times. Parents should know their kids' passwords and user names to all their social media accounts because if they do sneak out to meet someone or run away, that is one of the first things a detective will ask about and look at. Youths, you need to learn at an early age that this is non-negotiable, as there is no privacy when it involves your safety. Many missing juveniles have been located just by being able to look at their social media accounts.

If all else fails, parents, they still sell flip phones that can be used to only make phone calls.

11. *Suing*

A. Small Claims Or General Civil Court

Clerks can lose their job for giving you legal advice. There are no lawyers in Small Claims Court. If you want a lawyer, you must move it to General Civil Court, and yes, you will have to pay for your attorney.

Most people don't know how to sue someone or how to collect. First, you need to get your evidence together. Yes, text messages can be evidence. Print your text messages, copy your contracts or agreements, bring your tape-recorded messages and pictures that include screen shots—anything that proves your case. Have your witnesses write out what they saw. Make a copy! People tend to forget what they saw and/or said. Without your proof, you will most likely lose your case.

You'll need to have the name of the person you are suing, their address, phone number, date of birth, and eventually, social security number, place of employment, and a list of assets. You need to explain how and why they owe you money. Once you win and get your judgment, you will need their personal information for the courts to repossess their items.

B. Filing A Claim

For small claims, you need an *Affidavit and Claim Form*. It's about $1 at the court. You can also print the forms from online, but you need 4 copies for court.

C. Filing Fees (Subject To Change)

- Damage claims up to $600: $25 filing fee.
- Damage claims over $600 to $1,750: $45 filing fee
- Damage claims over $1,750 to $5,500: $65 filing fee
- General Civil Claim - Damage claims over $5,500: $150 filing fee

There is an additional $5 fee for electronic filing.

Fill out the form, giving the reason you're suing and a breakdown of how much you're suing for. You need to prove your damages, so no random amounts. Have some type of detailed list of what is owed.

You can hire a process server or have a friend take it to the person and hand-deliver it—*yes!* put it in their hand—then take the other copy back to the court. Remember, no lying. They can call that person in to testify that they really served the paperwork.

D. Judgments

Once you prove your case, you receive a Judgment. You must wait 21 days; then you can go back to the court and file a Writ of Garnishment to take their taxes or paychecks, garnish their bank accounts, or you can file a Seizure of Property to take their personal property for the debt that is owed. Their property will be auctioned so you can get the money, or you can request to keep the property.

Judgments are only good for 6 years, but you can file for an extension before the 6th year.

If they file bankruptcy, you need to file an Extension on Judgment so you can still collect. If they didn't include your Judgment in the bankruptcy, you can still collect.

If you sue someone and win, they have 21 days to appeal the magistrate's decision, whether they show up in court or not. What that means is, if they file a motion saying the amount is unfair, it will generally go to a judge. A judge will hear the case all over and can make changes to this case, lowering or raising the amount.

What you need to understand at this point is you may need witnesses to testify for you, and you will have to prove every aspect of your case over again. Then, the judge will render a decision. If you aren't happy with that decision, you can't file an appeal because the judge has the final say, but you can file a motion for reconsideration. If the judge changes his ruling, you must ask for the judgment to be in effect immediately. Otherwise, you have to wait the 21-day period. And, while you're there in court, get all pertinent information to collect on your suit, i.e., place of employment, social security number, etc.

The person you sued still can request a payment arrangement. The payment arrangement may be granted if they are working, but they will have to explain to the court where their money comes from and list all their assets and their bills. The payment arrangement may be denied if they are collecting assistance because that can't be garnished.

There is always a 21-day grace period for one to start collections. You must ask the judge on record for the personal information of the person you have sued because you can't complete the court forms without a social security number and date of birth. It will be hard to find out where they bank at or work without this information. You need to ask for everything while you are there because trying to get a Debtor's Exam will not always work, especially when they know they owe you. They just won't show up or will avoid being served.

If you ask for the extra information, you can file for a seizure of property, and the court will take their car or other possessions if there aren't any liens and sell it so you can redeem your money. Another tip is, if someone is on social security disability, unemployment, or some type of assistance, you can't garnish their income. But, if they work an under-the-table job, you can report them. You may want to tell them this because this may give them a reason to pay you rather than lose their income.

E. Extensions On Judgements And Beating Bankruptcy

People often don't know a judgment is generally good for 10 years, but if you haven't collected your money within the 10-year time frame, there are tricks to help. Most people don't realize that right before the judgment expires, you can file a Motion for Extension, giving you another 10 years to collect. Or, if the person you sued files bankruptcy, you still can collect after the 10 years because the judgment will always be good if you extend it.

For more information on tips on collections, sign up for our blog or webinars. Don't worry, you will always win.

***

12. How the Court System Works

A. Juvenile Court

(1) Juveniles are arraigned by a referee.

(2) Juvenile cases can get designated, which means they are charged like an adult but still held in Juvenile Court and Juvenile Jail.

(3) On certain charges, they can have a 5-day hold to be charged. *For example:* robbery, carjacking, murder 1 and 2, assault with intent, criminal sexual conduct (CSC) 1. Those are considered life offenses and minors can be charged as adults.

They can be held and housed until age 17. At age 17, they can be transferred to a regular jail or prison. The court system can keep them until they are 21.

(4) When a juvenile has a domestic issue, they only get one chance. After the first domestic violence charge, it will be on your permanent record, but you can try to get an Expungement.

(5) Juveniles are placed in what is considered baby jail, which is called Juvenile Detention.

(6) It is mandatory that a juvenile goes to school. School is in the Juvenile Center.

B. Adult Court

(1) When a crime is committed, someone contacts the police and is assigned a detective. They must complain and want justice.

(2) They tell the detective what happened, then write out what happened. This is called giving a statement.

(3) They must provide some type of proof of the crime.

(4) The detective does an investigation and writes up a Complaint, sending it to the prosecutor.

(5) The prosecutor reviews the Complaint and the evidence. If they have enough evidence to charge a person with the crime, they issue a Warrant. There needs to be enough proof to show a crime has been committed. The more proof they have, the easier it is to get a Warrant.

(6) The Warrant is entered into a national database, giving a description of you and the areas you go to, so the police can find you.

(7) The criminal is arrested.

(8) In most cases, the criminal must be formally charged (arraigned) within 72 hours of the arrest, or released. If the arrest is on a holiday, it may be 96 hours. When you get arrested, you should be prepared to sit for at least 72 hours.

(9) This is when you contact a bail bondsman—after you get arraigned. Their job is to discount the amount of money the court wants to release you from jail. Then you get an attorney.

(10) If you file a Complaint, you need to understand that, if you change your mind, it is still going to cost money and take a few months to get the case dropped, and sometimes, the police won't drop the case even if you want them to. It isn't as easy as it sounds.

(11) When a Complaint is filed, someone wants justice. There may be witnesses. Witnesses usually tend to pop up in cases.

NOTE: People don't just get arrested. The police aren't just trying to pick on you. You just finally got caught.

The reason you need to know how both juvenile and adult courts go is because, in certain types of cases, the court will charge a minor as an adult, so it is good for you to understand what is going on and how it works.

C. Getting Bond

(1) A judge or magistrate has to formally charge you (arraignment).

(2) They look at:

(a) Your past record (includes not showing up in court for tickets).

(b) The crime itself—whether there is probable cause a crime was committed.

(c) Your ties to the community. (Do you have a job? Do you rent or own? How long have you lived at your house?)

(d) The safety of the public—to determine what it will take to make sure you go back to court.

For example: If a magistrate or referee sets your bond at $10,000 cash surety, that means your parents will have to pay $1,000. Then they'll have to pay for you an attorney. Attorneys have a preset amount you have to pay to get them ***TO START*** working on your case. This is called a retainer. Then, as your case continues, you will have to make payments on the attorney fees until your case is completed and all fees are paid in full. So, where is all this money going to come from?

Let's just do some simple math. Let's say you live in a single-parent home (and your parent does not receive child support, or you live with both parents, but only one is working) and your parent makes $10 an hour. Mind you, minimum wage is around $8 an hour.

$10/hour x 8 hours/day	$80.00
$80/day x 5 days/week (does not include deductions for taxes or insurance)	$400.00
$400/WEEK X 4 WEEKS/MONTH	*$1,600.00*

Then subtract from that, the following monthly expenses (*figures are for purposes of illustration only and are actually on the low side*):

Rent	$600.00
Food	$250.00
Water, Electricity, Heat	$250.00
Phone, Cable, Auto Gas	$350.00
Sub-Total	*$1,450.00*

That would leave your parents with less than $150/month after all the expenses. *Remember, we did not deduct for taxes and insurance.* How could they afford to pay for your bond and attorney?

When you are a minor, you have to hope your parents have the money to post your bond while you fight your case. They will also have to hire you an attorney. This gets expensive. Kids never think about whether their parents have money or not. Maybe this is an off-week, where your parents don't get paid weekly. Will they have to borrow money to help you and get into more debt? How are they going to pay for these additional expenses and survive?

When youth get into trouble, they don't realize they will have to pay for the bond, possibly a tether, an attorney, time in jail, fines and costs, rehabilitation programs, and eventually, Expungements. These things can be very costly. *For example:*

Example of a Bond:	$5,000 Cash/Surety.
Bond:	$500 - $5,000
Tether:	$230 per month (Misdemeanor cases last around 3 months)
Attorney:	Just the retainer could start at $2000 down, which is not the complete payment for an attorney. (Hired attorneys charge $200 per hour. Court-appointed attorneys make around $10-15 per hour.)
Jail Time:	Approximately $150 per day (Normally takes 3 days to be arraigned.)
Fines and Costs:	Generally start at $300 and up. Depending on the charge.
Rehabilitation Programs:	Start at $250 and up.

Expungement:	$250 and up, depending if you do it yourself or hire an attorney.

I tell you this because, as a young person, if you don't understand how money works, you won't understand that if your parents have to bond you out of jail, they might not be able to come up with the money. Not to mention, you need to understand that you too need to be on the right path to handle money, especially if you want a nice life. One thing the system may not teach you is how not to get into too much debt because, when you really need money, you won't be able to get it.

I want you to see where you can help yourself by getting a job and saving your money just in case you need it, and how to use your money to get more money legally. It may take a little longer than fast money, but it works, and you won't have to look over your shoulder like you would if you're breaking the law. When you get fast money, eventually you get caught, and you won't be prepared for the cost of what it's going to take to get you out of trouble. That's why fast cash isn't worth it in the long run.

Credit is an important system that is a record of how you handle money. Your word. For you to get it, you borrow a certain amount of money and you agree to pay it back. The trick is to constantly keep a balance of less than 25% of your credit limit on your cards for your credit score to increase. It is a money and numbers game. If they see you can pay the money back every month and you aren't spending over your limit or paying late, your money balance will go up.

If you have a credit card with a limit of $300, that means you should keep a balance of $50 every month on that card to make your credit grow. How you break this down is, if $300 is the limit, you need to stay under the ¼ mark (which is $75) for you to increase your credit limit. It is a numbers game. It shows the credit card company you aren't broke by keep maxing your cards out and it shows them you still need them.

Then there is the credit pay period. A credit card reports 2 times a month to the credit bureaus. Most of the time it is at the middle of the month and the end, but you must ask your own company to stay on top of this. Then you need to play the money game. If your bill is due on the 1st of the month, then on the 15th of the month, they look at what you have used; so that's the high point of your spending. Then on the 28th of the month, you need to pay your balance down 80%. It shows you're responsible and in 3-to-6 months, they will increase your credit limit. It's not only important to pay your bills on time, but you also have to manage the amount of credit you use every month for your credit score to go up.

Your parents can get you a credit card in your name at age 13. You and your parents can start establishing credit for you, so when you're an adult, it will be easy to get more credit. But, you have to pay the credit card on time every month and you can't overspend.

This is learning how to balance your money and money management. If you can't pay your bills, call the company and make payment arrangements. If you don't, it will hurt you later.

D. Fines And The Costs For Sentencing

Based on the crime committed, all crimes have basic amounts that the court assesses to you. The following are the current court assessments after a conviction/plea (each jurisdiction is scheduled to change fees):

1. Crime Victims Fee: $75 for a misdemeanor per docket; $130 for a felony per docket.
2. Justice Assessment Fee (State): $68 minimum fee.
3. Court Administrative Fee: $50.
4. Pre-Sentence Report Fee: $100.
5. Court-Appointed Attorney Fee: $1,500 (depending on whether it's a simple plead out or a jury trial of several days).
6. Fine Of The Offense: Depends on the charge. (Look up a charge to insert the fee in your calculations.)
7. Monthly Probation Supervision Fee: $30.
8. Drug/Alcohol Testing Fee" $50.
9. Alcohol Tether/GPS Monitoring Fee: $200-$500 per month.
10. Restitution Fee: Depends on the crime or the victim.
11. Probation-Related Classes Fee:
    - Counseling: $150 per visit
    - Alternative Workforce Supervision Fee: $50 per visit (determined by county).
    - Batterers' Counseling Fee: $50 per session.
12. Suppressions is what the court systems don't tell you about how these things work, like:
    - HYTA: is now up to age 26, and once you have been sentenced, no criminal record will show up.
    - 7411 and Diversion: your criminal record shows up in a background check until you successfully complete your probation.

Add up everything up and this will give you an understanding of how much it would cost you to break the law. When you add up all this money, you could have bought a lot of necessary items.

E. The System's Trap

Unlike the police, lawyers, and judges, we have not been trained to know the rules. The system is set up so they are continuously informed of what is new in the law. They know how to follow the rules and what to look for when people break them. Then, when they charge you, that's when you find out about the new laws. This is why the system has an advantage over you.

F. The Court Process

(1) Every process starts in District Court, whether it is a misdemeanor or a felony.

(a) Arraignment: The court tells you what you are being charged with, then gives you a bond. Bond is supposed to be to make sure you show up to all your court dates, but some judges use it as a punishment. Is it fair you're being punished before you're even found guilty?

(b) Preliminary Exam: One of the most important court dates. You want to know why? This is where the prosecutor must show some of their evidence (just enough to get to the next stage) and they have to prove it (where you can get the charges dropped).

If they don't have enough evidence to prove Probable Cause, your case can be thrown out (dismissed). If they do have enough evidence, you either try to work out a plea deal, or you get bound over to Circuit Court if your case is a felony, where the above steps are repeated, and your bond can be raised or lowered. If your case is a misdemeanor, it stays in District Court and proceeds to trial.

You need to understand why your attorney may want to waive your Preliminary Exam. The Exam may allow a witness to make a statement that is now on record that will hurt your case in the long run. That is why it is important to know when to waive your Preliminary and to have an exceptionally good attorney. You don't want it to backfire.

(c) Plea Hearing: To work out a deal. (It takes more money to prove you are innocent versus taking a plea. That why there are so many convictions.)

(d) Trial:

i. Jury Trial: 6-to-12 people get to hear your case and decide if you are guilty. Remember, they are given rules to follow, but most of the time, they aren't using common sense to understand your case. These people don't live in your world, and many have never been convicted of a crime, so they will never truly understand your circumstances. *For example:* Why you would live in the inner city vs. the suburbs? What are the street rules? Some jurors may not be able to put themselves in your shoes, but they need to for you to get a fair trial.

ii. Bench Trial: The judge hears your case without a jury and decides your punishment.

(e) Sentencing: You get your punishment.

(2) Felony Process

(a) Arraignment: The court tells you what you are being charged with, then continues your bond from District Court or they can change your bond. That means they can raise or lower it.

(b) Pre-Trial Exam: This is where you negotiate, and if you can't negotiate, then it goes to trial. Your attorney can ask for an Evidentiary Hearing if they feel there was some constitutional violation.

(c) Trial: Same as Trial in Misdemeanor Process above.

(d) Sentencing: You get your punishment.

SOME PROCEDURES MAY BE DIFFERENT IN DIFFERENT AREAS OF THE COUNTRY, BUT WILL STILL BE VERY SIMILAR.

G. Sentencing Guidelines

The class of a crime is determined by the seriousness of the crime and your score:

- Crimes against a person
- Crimes against property
- Crimes involving drugs
- Crimes against public rules
- Crimes that don't keep the public safe
- Crimes that can hurt the public's trust

At sentencing, the court must consider the nature of the crime and the criminal's past, and the sentence must be equal to the seriousness of the crime.

The sentencing guidelines is a scale that rates the harshness of the crime. Important facts may include, among others:

1. The seriousness of the crime.
2. Factors not considered by the guidelines, such as:
    a. The relationship between the victim and the criminal;
    b. The criminal's behavior while in custody;
    c. Does the criminal care or is sorry (shows remorse); and,
    d. Can the criminal get better with rehabilitation.

The guidelines are a point system that show the court how they may sentence you. Even though you can Google the laws and guidelines, the judicial system makes it very hard for the average person to understand what's going on. That's why you need an attorney to go through the guidelines with you. Usually, there is room for your attorney to negotiate your charge, which would lower your points and give you less time. That's only if you have a good attorney who is willing to negotiate for you.

There are some cases, like drunk driving cases, where the best deal they can get is to let you keep your driver's license and do less than 90 days in jail. Know, of course, on a Drunk Driving 1 charge, you should try to get it reduced to an Impaired Driving charge so you can at least go to Canada. A drunk driving offense is not expungable and you can't go to Canada with a drunk driving offense.

1. Alternative Sentencing

ANYTHING BEATS GOING TO JAIL! The following is a list of alternative sentences to going to jail.

1. Drug Treatment Program: an inpatient or outpatient drug treatment, or participation in a drug treatment court.
2. Probation with any conditions required or authorized by law.
3. Residential probation.
4. Probation with jail.
5. Probation with special alternative incarceration.
6. Mental health treatment.
7. Mental health or substance abuse counseling.
8. Electronic monitoring–a tether.
9. Jail with work or school release—leave jail only to go to work or school.

10. Participation in a community corrections program.

11. Community service—picking up trash, for example.

12. Payment of a fine.

13. House arrest—you must stay in the house.

14. Diversion—you don't go to jail and you pay a fine. If you don't break the rules, you won't have anything on your record.

15. Home Youth Training Act (HYTA)—a sentence for someone who is under 26 years old, so the charges can come off their record after they have completed their probation and no criminal record will exist. This does not include capital punishment cases or drug offenses.

16. 7411—deferred sentence applies directly to drug crimes.

Yes, some judges will give you HYTA or 7411, and I have seen them given multiple times.

When you wear a tether, there are ways to trick the monitoring system, but if the tether doesn't work properly, what's the point of it?

H. Facing Your Consequences

The fact that you didn't know something was a crime doesn't mean you won't get in trouble for it. People say ignorance is bliss, meaning what you don't know won't hurt you. ***Wrong!*** Ignorance will not only hurt you, but ignorance of some things can kill you! The law says ignorance of the law is no excuse. As far as the law is concerned, the fact that you didn't know something was illegal is your problem and you should have learned it.

Something as small as getting a ticket and not dealing with the ticket can get you in more trouble.

1. You get a ticket.
2. You have around 14 days to pay it, or call and make a court date.
3. You don't pay it or go to your court date.
4. Within 2 weeks, you get a warning letter with some fines added onto the ticket.
5. 30 days later, you get a letter suspending your license.
6. 30 days later, you get a warrant out for your arrest.
7. You get arrested for driving while your license is suspended.

This could all have been prevented if you had just made an arrangement to take care of the ticket—like asking for a payment plan, or community service in the case of a misdemeanor— but you pushed the limits.

As a minor, no one tells you that when you get a ticket and you go to court, the court will make you post a bond for that ticket just to make sure you show back up to court. If you don't have the money to post bond right then, they can arrest you until you pay it. That's why it's important to always bring someone to court with you. Also, in certain courts, you can't carry a cellphone, so if they do lock you up, you won't be able to make a call right then and there.

***

13. Court Job Descriptions

Understand what the people do who work in the court system.

A. Defense Attorney: makes sure the court follows the law and works out the best deal for you.

B. Prosecutor: works for the court to prove you committed a crime and to protect the public's safety. They are supposed to find the truth, then seek justice.

C. Judge: listens to both the prosecutor's and the defense attorney's stories. If guilt is proven (see Jury Trial and Bench Trial above), punishes the criminal. ***NOTE:*** The judge has the final word ad can overturn a jury verdict.

D. Bailiff: makes sure the court stays safe.

E. Detective: checks out a Complaint and investigates to see if the law has been broken.

F. Clerk: files all court paperwork, and collects payments. Gives no legal advice.

G. Juror: listens to both sides of the story and decides who is telling the truth. Your responsibility as a juror is to look at the facts and evidence and decide if they support the charges. It isn't about what you know! It's about what has been proven! Don't overthink it!

H. Magistrate: person who listens to facts and judges issues (not always a lawyer).

I. Bail Bondsperson: gets a person out of jail and babysits them so they keep going back to court.

J. Tether Company: keeps track of your every movement for a nice price.

K. Pretrial Release: pretrial release personnel check out your past record and report to the judge if it would be safe to release you into public and you'll come back to court. (It sounds nice to get your loved one out for free, but do you *really* want a criminal out for free who isn't being monitored?)

L. Police: regulate the law and protect your safety.

M. Court Administrator: makes sure court employees are following the court rules.

N. Court Reporter: listens to the case and records everything said in court.

O. Referee: listens to both sides and tries to negotiate a deal.

P. Process Server: locates you and gives you court paperwork.

Q. Probation Officer: keeps a record and monitors what you do to make sure you aren't breaking the law, or they will have to send you back to jail.

***

14. Understanding The Police And Warrants

Breaking News: The government just gave all courts the right to charge the harshest punishment!

When a detective is working on a Warrant, their job is to try to get as much evidence as they can against you to show a crime has been committed (Probable Cause) to the prosecutor. This is the start of the story that will be told in court in a criminal case. In most cases, a person goes to the police and files a Complaint, telling the police their side of the story. The police then start to collect information by gathering evidence. Once they feel they have enough evidence, they may try to contact the criminal.

This is where it pays to understand your rights! Don't go in there without your parents and an attorney! The police will sometimes come at you in the nicest way possible. They will try to sweet-talk you into telling them your version of what happened. ***That is the biggest no-no!*** That's called ***giving a statement.*** It may not seem like a statement to you, but it is. Most people don't remember their right to ***shut up,*** or the fact that they don't have to answer anything. For your information, police don't have to read you your Miranda Rights up front, or at this point in time. It's your right not to go in to speak to the police. There is no Warrant for you at this point. Remember, they are trying to get a Warrant for you. Don't hand it to them!

Note: With Warrants, they have Priority Warrants, where they may not charge you right then, but they will come back and charge you later. That's why some people get released quickly.

A. What You Need To Know About Your Miranda Rights

(1) The police are ***not*** your friend when they have been called on you.

(2) You have the right to remain silent. ***Use it! Shut up! Don't say anything!***

(3) Everything you say can and will be used against you in a court of law.

(4) The police record everything you say so they can use it against you, even in the jail calls. There is nothing you can say that can help you out of this situation, so even if you think you're smart enough to get yourself out of this issue, ***don't say anything!***

The police's goal is to not let you walk out the police station a free person. Yes, they can and will lie to you. They may try to bully you, but that is a scare tactic to get evidence against you.

(5) You have the right to an attorney and they can be present when you are questioned. If you ask for an attorney, the police are not supposed to continue to ask you anything, but they'll still try. However, you are not magically given an attorney just because you ask for one! You have to call one yourself. Then, you need to sit silently and wait for him/her to get there.

An attorney's job is to protect you from saying the wrong thing to the police so they can't use it against you later. A good attorney will tell you, "Tell me what happened and I'll decide what to tell them for your protection."

(6) If you can't afford an attorney, one will be given to you. Most attorneys won't let you make a statement. However, a Public Defender won't be assigned to you until you are arraigned, and that means you can be held for up to 3 days in a jail cell before they have to arraign you, so be patient and be quiet. Everything is still being recorded! And, they can use your roommate as a witness if you tell them what happened. (P.S.: ***ALL PHONE CALLS ARE RECORDED AND CAN BE USED AGAINST YOU.***)

Probable Cause is enough proof that a crime has been committed—*for example:* videos, copies of paperwork, weapons with matching fingerprints, testimonials from witnesses—then they build the story behind that.

Showing is knowing! It isn't good enough just to *know* your rights. You must *show* you know your rights. Be nice. No arguing. Stay calm, ask what law(s) you have broken, and ask if you're free to go or if you're being detained.

B. Snitching

(1) Snitching on Yourself

Times are different than when your parents were growing up. Some of them had enough sense to do their dirt all by themselves—they didn't want any witnesses.

But, now, you tell on yourself. You post on Facebook, Snapchat, Instagram, TikTok, and more, everything you do.

For example: You take pictures of yourself with weed and money, then you post it on your social media sites. What is that saying? I'll tell you: "Look! That fool has lots of drugs and cash. Let's rob him. We know he doesn't have a job." And you don't seem to realize the police make fake profiles to monitor you. So, you get someone requesting you as a friend. You aren't sure if you know them, but their picture is cute. It may be a setup. Then when you get pulled over, you claim they're setting you up and harassing you. No, dummy, you showed them everything you've been doing and now they're trying to catch you up.

You don't have a job, but you're always posting money on your social media pages. Do you think the police think you hit the lottery? LOL. Or, that you're doing something illegal? Because when you're getting money legally, you don't post it on social media. Hopefully, you're saving it. Things need to add up, or eventually, the system is going to get you. Some things are meant to be kept to yourself.

(2) Snitching on Your Friends

Most young people think if you didn't do anything wrong, they should not be able to charge you. Unfortunately, it isn't true in some cases.

For example: You are with a friend and you two go to the store. That friend decides to steal something. You are still going to get into trouble, even if you had no clue what your friend was doing. There's an old saying: Birds of a feather flock together. That means if your friends steal, so do you. It may not be true, but you're going down too. You will have to prove your innocence, and the way the system is set up, the first person who talks, usually gets the better deal. So, even if you aren't a snitch, it's going to be you or them, and maybe they have parents who are saying to their child, "Tell, because you have a future ahead of you and you don't need any record." So, don't expect them to be silent or to tell the truth!

C. True Or False

		T	F
(1)	Your juvenile record can be used against you as adult.	_____	_____
(2)	It's a crime to take a selfie with a gun.	_____	_____
(3)	A police officer can't arrest a minor.	_____	_____
(4)	If you have a fight with your parent, it is mandatory 20 hours in jail.	_____	_____
(5)	Teachers can't go through your locker.	_____	_____
(6)	You can't be arrested for just being with someone who commits a crime.	_____	_____
(7)	You can be charged as an adult at age 12.	_____	_____
(8)	It's a crime to lie to the police.	_____	_____
(9)	If you pull a girl's bra or touch a minor's butt or crotch, you can be charged as a sex offender.	_____	_____
(10)	You can be charged criminally for a Facebook challenge.	_____	_____
(11)	You can get 25 years in prison for stealing a car.	_____	_____
(12)	If you get in trouble in school, it can't turn into trouble with the law.	_____	_____
(13)	You can legally carry your friend's identification.	_____	_____
(14)	It's a crime to give a friend an aspirin or a pain pill.	_____	_____
(15)	It's a crime to stop someone from using their phone.	_____	_____
(16)	It is possible for a minor to get raped in jail.	_____	_____
(17)	It is a crime to have sex if you're both minors.	_____	_____
(18)	You can get charged with a crime even if you didn't know it was a crime.	_____	_____
(19)	Touching or being around someone smoking drugs can get into your system.	_____	_____

When it comes to real crime, you may break the law several times before you get caught. That doesn't make it right! There are many police officers who will give you a warning, but your luck will run out. When you're a minor, you may not realize that sometimes the crimes you commit will fall on your parents. What that means is, your parents can get sued and/or go to jail because you broke the law. Would you have committed the crime if you knew your parents, who are working hard to take care of you, would no longer be able to do those little extras for you because you made a bad choice?

In many cases, when you do minor crimes at school, just the school punishes you, but there are crimes where you can also get in trouble with the law. They have incorrigibility programs, which are programs for when you keep getting in trouble and the school, your parents, or the courts don't seem to think you are getting any better. They can have a court hearing and punish you with fines, probation, counseling, community service, boot camps, or juvenile detention (jail).

True example: A 13-year-old girl was sitting at her desk in class when the boy behind her kept pulling her bra strap. She asked him to stop several times, but he wouldn't. She went to her teacher and told him. He told the boy to leave her alone and told her to go back to her seat. The boy kept pulling at her bra strap until it opened. The girl was so embarrassed, she turned around and punched the boy in his nose, causing him to have a terrible nosebleed.

The parents of both the children were called to the school. The boy's parents got there first. They wanted the principal to call the police and charge the girl with assault. Then the girl's mother finally got there.

She listened to the boy's story, then asked the teacher, "Is that what happened?"

The teacher replied, "Yes."

Then she asked her daughter if that was what happened. Her daughter said, "Yes, that is what happened."

The girl's mother said to the principal, "What are you going to do?"

The principal said, "I'm going to have to expel your daughter for a few days."

The mother said, "And what are you going to do to the boy?"

They all looked confused. Then the boy's parents said, "See, this is why we are going to press charges against your daughter."

The girl's mother said, "Okay, let's call the police right now, but I want you to understand that your son kept sexually assaulting my daughter and the teacher assisted him in the assault. I have no problem with the police charging my daughter for defending herself, but I will be pressing charges against your son, so he can be charged with criminal sexual conduct and he will have to register as a sexual predator because that is exactly what he is."

The girl's mother told the principal she would have her attorney contact the school because she planned to sue them. The mother of the boy started crying and begging the girl's mother to please not press charges; they didn't want any trouble.

In this story, you see how easy a school situation can turn into a legal situation. A lot of minors don't see that if their parents get locked up, they could lose what they have. No freedom could mean losing their job, their car, and their home. More importantly, you could get lost in the system, and for what? You did something you know you shouldn't have. *For example:* If you keep skipping school, they can lock your parents up for your truancy. If they are locked up, who is going to take care of you? They will put you in the foster care system. Everything you do can come back to hurt you ***AND OTHERS.***

***

15. Tips On How To Hire An Attorney

You may have a serious case where you need to hire an 'A' attorney—also known as the pit-bull attorney—who is seasoned. They are well-connected and respected within the system, and they are expensive. The reason you would need an attorney like this is because you are guilty as sin and/or you are facing some serious time—like a life sentence—and you need their expertise. With an 'A' attorney, the judge and prosecutor already know they'll have a hell-of-a-fight with this case because this type of attorney isn't looking for a deal. They are generally looking for the complete win and a dismissal of the case.

Then you have the "B' attorneys. They have good experience but aren't as well-connected as the 'A' attorneys. They're still working their way up the ladder. They'll probably charge you half the amount the 'A' attorneys charge, but will still be able to get the same results as the 'A' attorneys. So, the difference between 'A' and 'B' attorneys is the amount of experience they have, their connections, and the price.

Then the 'C' attorneys may not have any of the connections, but they will fight hard for you because they are trying to get the connections and build a reputation for themselves. They'll probably charge half what the 'B' attorneys charge, and they can come up with good results, maybe not as good as an 'A' or 'B' attorney, but still good, especially for the price.

Now 'B' and 'C' attorneys are recommended for cases where you may be looking at up 15 years. These attorneys may be able to do some serious negotiating for your case. The 'D' attorneys may be considered as attorneys who are just trying to get deals—not really trying to go the distance with the case. You may need them to deal with a ticket or some type of misdemeanor—nothing too big, where your life and a lot of time could be taken from you.

‘A’ attorneys may charge $10,000-$20,000, plus.

‘B’ attorneys may charge $5,000-$10,000.

‘C’ attorneys may charge $2,500-$5,000.

‘D’ attorneys may charge $750-$1.500.

(These are approximate figures.)

Court-appointed attorney get money from the government to get your evidence, versus a hired attorney has to get the money from you to hire specialists. That's part of the high cost of a hired attorney. You can get a court-appointed attorney for the first few weeks, then fire them by getting your own attorney, and they can give your new attorney your evidence. This will lower your cost of a hired attorney. Why do you think these attorneys cost so much? It's the little expenses that you pay extra for the little expenses. *For example,* lie detector tests, private investigators, phone records, specialists to retest lab results, specialists to make sure evidence was not tampered with.

When hiring an attorney, you do not want to hire the first one you speak to. Check on several attorneys. You don't want to hire the one who just tells you what you want to hear. You would not just buy the first car you see; you would test drive several before buying. You can go into court and ask the judge to give you a 2-to-3 week extension so you can hire the right attorney.

Juveniles and parents have the right to fire an attorney at any time and get a new one. If an attorney is threatening you to quit, you can file a Grievance and tell the judge so the judge can stop them, especially until you find a new attorney. Don't allow anyone to bully you.

When looking to hire an attorney, remember their job is to make your story believable—in other words, who can tell the best lies to the judge and jury. So, of course they will tell you what you want to hear to get you to hire them. Pay attention to that. Also, find the right type of attorney. Just because they practice law doesn’t mean they are good in the area you need them in. For example, you wouldn’t hire a civil attorney who sues people and specializes in insurance, medical, contract, or real estate law to represent you in a criminal case. You need a criminal attorney. Make sure you hire the right type of attorney. All areas of law are not the same. Here are the different types of attorneys:

- Intellectual property attorney: deals with copyrights.
- Family law attorney: handles divorce or child support family matters.
- Estate law attorney: death benefits,
- Real estate attorney: deals with foreclosures,
- Personal injury attorney: deals with physically damages, possibly from a 0car accident, or defamation of character.

- Malpractice law attorney: medical problems.
- Business, labor, tax, bankruptcy, immigration, Constitution law, environmental, civil litigation, and finally criminal attorneys.

***

6. Top Ten Crimes for Adults

1. Drugs
2. Assault
3. Driving Under the Influence (DUI)
4. Home Invasion, Larceny, Breaking & Entering, Retail Fraud
5. Carrying a Concealed Weapon (CCW)
6. Carjacking
7. Criminal Sexual Conduct (CSC)
8. Fraud
9. Robbery & Unarmed Robbery
10. Obstruction

PARENTS SHOULD KNOW: If you aren't paying attention to your children, it could cause you to go to jail. If your child is skipping school, ***WHETHER YOU KNOW IT OR NOT,*** the schools have special truancy officers who put the parents in jail and charge them with a misdemeanor for their children missing too much school.

PARENTS ALSO NEED TO UNDERSTAND: *Your child may be getting sexually assaulted at school, and you have the right to press charges.* It is a crime for a child to snap another child's bra strap, flash another child, and even try to pull down a child's pants. Even though you may think it's harmless, it is considered sexual assault. ***Protect your child!***

A. Catch-22 Of The Law

What do you mean, they're locking people up for showing evidence?

The law is trying to punish people who video record fights. But, what they don't tell them is, if they video and try to help stop the threat, they won't get charged. On the other hand, if they publish it, they want to charge them with accessory to the crime. Then, if you call the police for help when the crime is being committed, they tell you to stay away and don't get hurt. Which one is it: help or run?

17. Crime Time Chart

In your phone or computer, Google or go to the state of ____________ (*choose a state*) to look up the actual laws by typing in the name of the law in the search box. For example: Type *'Michigan law on larceny'* in your search box. It will come up www.legislature.mi.gov/doc Section 750.356, the laws on stealing.

This is only a guide for the courts to use. Since it is the judge's decision, you could get less time.

Charge	**Per *Attorneys***
Aggravated Assault and/or Battery	1 year
Aiding and Abetting	2-4 years
Animal Cruelty	Up to 6 months
Armed Robbery	Life
Assault w/Dangerous Weapon	2-4 years
Assault w/Intent to Commit Murder	6-10 years
Breaking & Entering Vehicle w/Damage to Vehicle	2-5 years
Breaking and Entering w/Intent	2-10 years
Breaking & Entering w/Intent to Commit a Felony	10 years
Breaking & Entering w/o Intent	5 years
Bribery	8-10 years
Carjacking	20 years
Carrying Concealed Weapon (CCW)	2-5 years
Carrying a Weapon w/Unlawful Intent	2-5 years
Checks w/o an Account	Up to 5 years
Computers, Using to Commit Crime	1-5 years
Child Endangerment	1 year, unless prior, Then 7 years
Child Pornography	2-5 years

Charge	Per *Attorneys*
Child Support, Failure to Pay	Up to 5 years
Cocaine, Heroin, Methamphetamine < 50 Grams	No jail up to 3 times
Conspiracy	Up to 5 years
Criminal Sexual Conduct 1 (Rape) CSC	Life
Criminal Sexual Conduct 2	15 years
Criminal Sexual Conduct 3	15 years
Criminal Sexual Conduct 4	2 years
Cyber-Bullying	1-15 years w/fine of $1,000-$15,000
Drunk Driving 3	1-5 years
Embezzlement	1-20, depending on amount
Escape from Jail	1-4 years
Fake License Tags	5 years
False Pretenses–20,000 or More Attempts	1-6 years
Felony Firearm	Mandatory 2 years
Felon in Possession (of a weapon)	5 years
Financial Transaction Device	1-4 years
Fleeing and Eluding	2-15, depending on degree
Forgery	Up to 5 years
Fraud	5-7 years
Hit and Run	1-15, depending on damage
Home Invasion 1	2-6 years
Human Trafficking	10 years to Life

Charge	Per *Attorneys*
Identity Theft	Up to 5 years
Kidnapping	Up to 20 years
Larceny (Stealing Property from a Person)	Up to 5 years
Mail and Wire Fraud	Up to 20 years
Maintaining a Drug House	2-3 years
Malicious Destruction of Personal Property	1-4 years
Motor Vehicle Unlawful Use	Up to 5 years
Murder	Life
Obstruction of Justice	2 years
Operate-License-Allow Person to Operate Up to 2nd Offense	Up to 5 years
Operating Intoxicated/Impaired/ Controlled Substance	1-5 years
Perjury	5 years
Possession of a Firearm	2-5 years
Receiving & Concealing Property	3-5 years
Receiving Stolen Property over $100	6-10 years
Resisting and Obstructing Justice	1-2 years
Retail Fraud 1	Up to 2 years
Retail Fraud 3	Less than 1 year
Solicitation, Child	4 years
Stalking	1-15 years
Theft	1-7 years, stealing goods
Threatening an Official (Police Officer, Judge)	2 years

Charge	**Per *Attorneys***
Treason	Life
Unarmed Robbery	15 years
Unlawful Driving Away Auto (UDAA)	6-10 years
Uttering & Publishing	Up to 3 years
Violating Parole, Probation, or Recognizance Bond	2-3 years
Weapons	1-6 years
Welfare Fraud	Up to 3 years
Witness Intimidation	Up to 5 years

This crime chart is based on first-time offenses. The time on any charge is negotiable. These charges are based on the crime being a felony. Some of these crimes can be broken down to misdemeanors. It is the judge's decision for your punishment. (THE INTENT OF THE CRIME IS WHAT GETS YOU!)

Most people do not think about who they hurt when they commit crimes. Have you ever asked yourself, "Who am I hurting?", especially when you think it may be a faceless crime. A faceless crime means you don't directly see or deal with someone to commit the crime, like credit card fraud. You may think the crime affects only you because when you get caught you're the only person in trouble, but it goes deeper than that. The first thing a criminal probably thinks when they are committing a crime is that they probably won't get caught, but as we can see statistically, that is wrong. Maybe they didn't get caught that time, but criminals rarely weigh their chances. Then there are all the people it affects, including their family and friends, because they have to come up with money to get them out of jail, pay for attorneys, put money on the phones to talk to them, put money on their commissary. They are victims also. Not that criminals really care about anyone else, but if it happened to their family, they would be upset.

What about the stores? If you keep taking from these places, it affects everyone because this is why their prices are so high. Of course, they don't think at that moment of how they have to come back to the real world and try to get a job against people who have a clean record so they seem more trustworthy. Criminals don't think about trying to go to college and having problems with housing or financial aid. They can't travel out of the country because they can't get a passport. In many states, they have trouble voting because some people think convicted criminals voices don't count, but every voice counts, especially if you want something done, you have to change it. Then you give up your Fourth

Amendment rights, one of the most important rights, so if you are on any type of probation or parole, you give up this right.

The police or a probation/parole officer does not need a warrant to harass and search you, your home, and any vehicle you are in. Then you have your creditability. You have none! No one will trust you, not even the streets, because they don't really know if you were a snitch. The streets will always side-eye you because your character is flawed. You are not TRUSTWORTHY. Regardless of whether you did it for a good cause in your mind, the world won't look at you the same.

***

18. New Crimes The Youths Are Committing

If you are underage (a minor), you can still be charged as an adult if you commit a crime, or if an adult has you commit the crime. There are courts that have charged youths as young as 12 years old as adults. You need to think: If you're about to do something that will you get in trouble with your parents, or that will embarrass them, then ***DON'T DO IT! IT'S PROBABLY A CRIME! JUST REMEMBER, IT'S YOUR BUTT ON THE LINE.***

A. How Is Bullying/Cyber-Bullying Punished?

In addition to the consequences incurred under school policy, someone who commits an act of bullying may also face criminal penalties.

Depending on the specific conduct involved, bullying and cyber-bullying may be prosecuted. The defense to cyber-bullying is free speech and if it's proven it wasn't really a threat.

B. Stalking

Stalking is usually a misdemeanor, and incurs a fine of up to $1,000, up to 1 year in jail, or both. However, if the victim is younger than 18 years old at the time of the offense, and the defendant is 5 or more years older than the victim, the offense is a felony. Penalties include a fine of up to $10,000, up to 5 years in prison, or both. The judge can also place a person convicted of stalking on probation for up to 5 years, including an order to refrain from contacting the victim during that time.

(1) Aggravated Stalking

Aggravated stalking is a felony, and incurs a fine of up to $10,000, up to 5 years in jail, or both. However, if the victim is younger than 18 years old at the time of the offense and the defendant is 5 or more years older than the victim, penalties increase to a fine of up to $15,000, up to 10 years in prison, or both. The judge can also place a person convicted of aggravated stalking on probation for at least 5 years (up to 10 years), and will include an order to refrain from contacting the victim during that time.

C. Posting Electronic Messages Without Consent

This offense is a felony, and incurs a fine of up to $5,000, up to 2 years in prison, or both. However, when the crime occurs in violation of a restraining order, when it involves a credible threat to harm or kill the victim (or a member of the victim's family), and in other similar specified circumstances, penalties increase to a fine of up to $10,000, up to 5 years in prison, or both.

D. Facts

(1) If you urinate or defecate in public (outside of a restroom—*for example,* like in the bushes), that's a crime. It is a misdemeanor, but if someone sees your genitals out in public, then you can be charged for a sex crime. You can be charged as a sex offender. If you are charged as a sex offender, you will have to register monthly for the rest of your life. You will be banned from certain type of events because it is illegal for sex offenders to be around minors. If you are charged with a sex crime and you are a minor, you can't go to school with other children. You will have to be home schooled or go to jail.

If you are an adult, you may lose custody of your children, and you can't go on field trips.

Juveniles can be held for up to 1 year to rehabilitate themselves.

(2) If your friend steals someone's cellphone and they bring it to you to hide for them, it doesn't matter if you know they stole it or not. If the police track the phone to you, you are going to get arrested for receiving and concealing stolen goods. See, young people don't know what technology the world has that sets them up, and they don't know enough to be prepared for life. That's why I'm trying to prepare you.

E. Are These Real Crimes?

		Y	N
(1)	Bullying?	_____	_____
(2)	Cutting someone's hair without their permission?	_____	_____
(3)	Fighting in public and pushing someone?	_____	_____
(4)	Sneaking out the house after curfew?	_____	_____
(5)	Hanging out of a car?	_____	_____
(6)	Cutting class and skipping school?	_____	_____
(7)	Urinating in public?	_____	_____
(8)	Taking someone's bicycle?	_____	_____
(9)	Taking someone's backpack from their locker?	_____	_____
(10)	Drawing on the bathroom wall?	_____	_____
(11)	Impersonating another person?	_____	_____
(12)	Sending fake email information?	_____	_____
(13)	Using someone's Bridge card, with or without their permission?	_____	_____
(14)	Writing a check when you have no money in your account?	_____	_____
(15)	Pulling a fire alarm?	_____	_____
(16)	Calling in a bomb threat?	_____	_____
(17)	Entering a vacant building?	_____	_____
(18)	Being around or having drugs (marijuana, heroin, opiates, cocaine, crack)?	_____	_____
(19)	Carrying a pocket knife?	_____	_____
(20)	Running from the police?	_____	_____
(21)	Running away from a noncustodial parent's home?	_____	_____
(22)	Holding stolen goods for a friend?	_____	_____
(23)	Driving a car without the owner's permission?	_____	_____
(24)	Staying at a friend or family's house without your parents' permission?	_____	_____
(25)	Refusing to move when ordered by an officer?	_____	_____
(26)	Violating a park curfew?	_____	_____
(27)	Shoplifting?	_____	_____
(28)	Keying a car and cutting tires?	_____	_____
(29)	Egging someone's car?	_____	_____
(30)	Using a friend or parent's debit or credit card, with or without their permission?	_____	_____

		Y	N
(31)	Returning to a store after being banned?	____	____
(32)	Having an adult buy you alcohol?	____	____
(33)	Giving alcohol to an underage minor?	____	____
(34)	Flashing/mooning and indecent exposure?	____	____
(35)	Having a weapon (brass knuckles, pocket knife, nunchucks, taser, gun)?	____	____
(36)	Having pepper spray?	____	____
(37)	Having a small amount of marijuana?	____	____
(38)	Chewing or smoking tobacco at school?	____	____
(39)	Giving a kid tobacco?	____	____
(40)	Walking home after curfew?	____	____
(41)	Damaging a mailbox?	____	____
(42)	Phone pranking?	____	____
(43)	Having a bicycle you know is stolen?	____	____
(44)	Hanging onto or out of a moving car?	____	____
(45)	Speeding out of a parking lot?	____	____
(46)	Lying to the police about your age?	____	____
(47)	Driving a car without the owner's permission?	____	____
(48)	Drinking alcohol?	____	____
(49)	Altering a phone, video game, or firestick?	____	____
(50)	Cashing someone else's check in your account?	____	____

ALL THE ABOVE ARE CRIMES and are not only punishable to minors, but the system can charge your parents too.

Sometime people don't realize when they break the law thinking they have done one crime, but when they get charged, it is more than one crime. The system is allowed to charge you with more than one charge, and this is one way how people have more than one felony or misdemeanor on their record. You generally can only get one felony removed off your record. You might get lucky and get 2 off.

For example: You steal a car and end up driving into another city. When you get pulled over, you're also in another county. You will get charged with stealing a car or joyriding, and fleeing and eluding the police if you try to outrun the police, but since you got caught in another county, you will be charged in that other county too. So, in this example, you will get 4 felonies, not to mention your parents could lose their insurance on the car because the insurance company won't insure a car with an illegal minor driving it, whether there was an accident or not.

Another example: James is a teenage boy and he's a little strapped for cash. He has a part-time job, so he gets on Facebook, Instagram, Snapchat, and Twitter, and asks, *Hey, does anyone have any food stamps I can buy?* Some lady replies, *Yes, inbox me when and where I can meet you.* She has 3 kids and she needs some extra cash, but she doesn't know it's illegal to sell her food stamps and for him to buy them. They meet up.

Months go by. James graduates and goes to get a better job. He gets the job, passes the drug test, and goes to get his background check done at the State police office . . . and two officers arrest him. James has no clue what's going on. He's being charged with felony welfare fraud. You can't use or buy anyone's food stamps or Bridge card.

Some people don't realize the government has a special police force that watches the internet (like Facebook), cellphones, and video records to see if people are breaking the law. This is why people get caught doing crimes in many places like stores and on social media.

When you commit crimes of theft, the outcome is a bigger problem than you think because things that are stolen have to be replaced. While it is being replaced, the companies who make or sell it raise their prices; this is why items go up in price. So, you may think it isn't important that you're stealing something cheap, but it breaks down in the long run and hurts everyone's money because now it cost more.

The fact is, as a minor, you may not understand how these things work and how they apply to you, so here is a simple explanation. When your parents work, they get money to take care of you. That means, this money is used for everything: to feed you; buy your clothes; have a home, a car, and put gas in the car; pay bills so you can bathe, watch television, turn on the lights; and more. These things are not free, so when you ask your parents to buy you things like a cellphone, they have to work to buy it and pay the bill to keep it on. Even as a minor, you should try to get a job to have our own money so you can buy some of these things for yourself, or at least help your parents buy them for you.

For example: You have a job cutting grass. You get paid $20 for every yard you cut, but after every 3 yards you cut, you need to fill up with gas. If you factor in the gas to fill up your lawnmower is $6, you're actually making $18 for every yard you cut. This means you would have to cut 6 yards to be able to go in half with your parents to buy a $200 pair of Jordans.

F. Estimated Number Of Juvenile Arrests, 2015

Please review the information on the next couple of pages. Information provided by the Office of Juvenile Justice and Delinquency Prevention (OJJDP) https://www.ojjdp.gov/ojstatbb/crime/qa05101.asp?qa

		Percent change		
Most Serious Offense	**Number of Juvenile Arrests**	**2006-15**	**2011-15**	**2014-15**
Total	921,600	-56%	-37%	-10%
Violent Crime Index	n/a	n/a	n/a	n/a
Murder and nonnegligent manslaughter	800	-38%	-6%	4%
Rape [1]	n/a	n/a	n/a	n/a
Robbery	18,500	-47%	-22%	-5%
Aggravated assault	28,600	-53%	-30%	-5%
Property Crime Index	208,800	-48%	-38%	-11%
Burglary	35,600	-57%	-43%	-12%
Larceny-theft	156,000	-44%	-39%	-12%
Motor vehicle theft	14,600	-58%	4%	15%
Arson	2,700	-66%	-45%	-14%
Nonindex				
Other assaults	131,300	-47%	-31%	-6%
Forgery and counterfeiting	1,000	-71%	-35%	-12%
Fraud	4,500	-39%	-13%	5%
Embezzlement	600	-57%	42%	26%
Stolen property (buying, receiving, possessing)	10,400	-51%	-22%	0%
Vandalism	41,700	-64%	-39%	-8%
Weapons (carrying, possessing, etc.	19,300	-59%	-32%	-7%
Prostitution and commercialized vice	600	-62%	-40%	-21%
Sex offenses (except forcible rape and prostitution)	n/a	n/a	n/a	n/a
Drug abuse violations	99,100	-50%	-33%	-12%
Gambling	500	-78%	-51%	-18%
Offenses against the family and children	3,400	-36%	-3%	0%
Driving under the influence	6,600	-67%	-35%	-5%
Liquor law violations	43,100	-69%	-51%	-19%
Drunkenness	5,500	-66%	-52%	-15%
Disorderly conduct	71,300	-66%	-49%	-12%
Vagrancy	1,100	-78%	-41%	13%
All other offenses (except traffic)	167,700	-56%	-37%	-10%
Curfew and loitering	44,800	-71%	-42%	-16%
Runaways*	n/a	n/a	n/a	n/a

1 Beginning in 2013, the FBI broadened the definition of rape, removing the phrase “forcible” from the offense name and description. The new definition of rape is: Penetration, no matter how slight, of the vagina or anus with any body part or object, or oral penetration by a sex organ of another person, without the consent of the victim. The new definition includes the NIBRS offenses of rape, sodomy, and sexual assault with an object.

Law enforcement agencies may submit data on rape arrests based on either the new or legacy definition of rape. Due to differences in agency reporting practices, national estimates for the offenses of “rape” and “sex offenses” are not available after 2012. Additionally, estimates for the Violent Crime Index (which included “forcible rape”) are not shown after 2012 as this category is no longer compatible with prior years.

*As of data year 2010, national estimates of running away are no longer available.

Internet citation: OJJDP Statistical Briefing Book. Online. Available: http://www.ojjdp.gov/ojstatbb/crime/qa05101.asp?qaDate=2015. Released on March 27, 2017.

Data Source: Arrest estimates for 1980-2014 developed by the Bureau of Justice Statistics and disseminated through “Arrest Data Analysis Tool.” Online. Available from the <a href=http://www.bjs.gov/index.cfm?ty=datool&surl=/arrests/index.cfm>B

Arrest estimates for 2015 developed by the National Center for Juvenile Justice based on data published in the FBI's 2015 Crime in the United States report [Tables 29, 39, and 40]. These are <b>preliminary</b> estimates that will be updated upon release of final estimates on the Bureau of Justice Statistics’ Arrest Data Analysis Tool.

19. Drug Usage Chart

This chart shows how long drugs stay in your system.

Drug	Urine	Hair	Blood	Saliva
Marijuana	15-30 days	90 days	90 days	3 days
Cocaine	5-15 days	90 days	5-15 days	5 days
Heroin	3 days	90 days	1 day	5 days
Ecstasy	2-5 days	90 days	24 hours	5 days
Methamphetamine	3-5 days	90 days	1-3 days	1-4 days
Molly	2-5 days	90 days	2-5 days	1-5 days

Kids don't understand that just by touching certain drugs, they can get into your system and you can test positive for the drugs for 90 days. Schools can test kids on a regular basis if they think a child is doing drugs.

It is important to know the new laws in Michigan about medical marijuana. One law is people under the age of 21 cannot use or possess marijuana. Another law is adults cannot use marijuana in front of a child 16 or younger. It is considered child endangerment.

The next law is you do not have the right to have marijuana or a gun at the same time. It is one or the other. So, if you get caught with a weapon, even though you are open carrying, or you have a carrying pistol license, and you have marijuana on you, you will now be charged with a crime, and vice versa. If you, for some reason, commit a crime and you have marijuana on you or in your system and you have a gun, you will get charged with a crime.

You are not allowed to drive while under the influence of drugs. If you get stopped and you've been smoking marijuana, you will be charged the same as drunk driving. Even though the legal limit for drunk driving is .08, the current legal limit for marijuana in your system is zero tolerance until this State can come up with a limit. You cannot have it in your system and drive, or operate any equipment with it in your system, or you will be charged with operating under the influence of drugs (OUID). The third time, you get charged with an OUID, it is a felony, just like with drunk driving.

- Even if you have a license/prescription to possess marijuana, you must keep it in a locked box when transporting it.

- A lot of employers are now drug testing immediately after an interview, so you won't have an opportunity to go clear any drugs out of your system.

20. Things You Need To Know, Especially If You Don't Break The Law

Ask yourself: Do you think the police care that you didn't know you were breaking the law? The answer is ***NO! IGNORANCE HAS NOTHING TO DO WITH INNOCENCE.*** The point is you did something illegal and now you have to deal with it.

Do you understand it is better to just get a ticket from the police than to be ***DEAD RIGHT?!*** Remember, the power a police officer has. They have the right to protect themselves, and at any time, if they feel you pose a threat, they can shoot you. ***SO, DON'T BE DUMB. TAKE THE TICKET AND FIGHT IT LATER IN COURT!***

If you have a Concealed Pistol License (CPL), there are certain areas where you can carry your gun. You cannot carry in a school zone or in a courthouse, for instance. This is why there are harsher penalties if you are found carrying weapons in these areas.

If you have a medical marijuana card, you have the right to buy marijuana and go home to smoke it. You don't have the right to smoke it in your car or at the park. That is illegal and can get you arrested for driving under the influence (DUI) or operating under the influence (OUI). If you are a minor, you still need to know this because, if someone is doing this around you, the penalty is doubled.

Many teens see their parents or other adults smoke marijuana and they think it is legal. The fact is it is not. It is very much illegal and against the law if you do not have a proper medical marijuana card. Also, some parents who have a medical marijuana card may not want to smoke in their homes, so they smoke in their cars. Then what happens is, the minor child drives their car and gets pulled over; they are searched and arrested. The children need to know how to handle the police in this situation by telling the officer it isn't their car, they don't have any drugs in the car, and they do not consent to a search without a warrant. Then they can call their parents and an attorney, so the attorney can explain they are not breaking the law by being in a car that smells like marijuana.

If you've never committed a crime, how would you know you're being set up? You wouldn't. That's why you think the law is on your side. LOL. That's why you need to know the one thing to say before answering any questions by anyone: ***I need my parents and an attorney, and I'll wait until they get here before we proceed.***

The more innocent you are, the quicker you need to get an attorney! If you are arrested, even if you have done absolutely nothing wrong, it would be wise to ask for an attorney anyway—even if it's just to explain what you know about the situation—because some people get nervous and scared and intimidated when speaking to the police. Sometimes, because they are scared, they get confused when speaking to the police. You don't want to get in trouble for mixing up what really happened because you were scared and confused.

Remember: Everything you say can and will be used against you!

You get pulled over and you have no clue what the speed limit is. Ask why you were pulled over, then calmly and quietly accept the ticket. ***You are never supposed to argue for any reason!*** If you take the ticket without saying anything else and you decide to fight it in court, you won't be surprised to find out you gave a statement you didn't realize you were giving ***and*** it was recorded.

This goes hand-in-hand with when you're being questioned by the police. Every time, whether you're innocent or guilty, you must know this: ***Don't answer any questions! Keep asking for a lawyer until one is provided!***

Here's how that conversation should go:

- "What's your name?"
  Give your name. Then say, "I need my parents and a lawyer", and don't say anything else until they arrive!
- "Do you know what you're here for?"
  "I need my parents and a lawyer."
- "If you're innocent, you don't have anything to hide."
  "Am I free to go? If not, I need my parents and a lawyer."

Do you get the point?! You have nothing to say, other than your name, except, ***"I need my parents and a lawyer!"***

The young generation listens to a lot of music and they can repeat all the words, but they still don't understand it, so let me break it down to you. Jay-z' *99 Problems* song came out in 2004. I'm going to explain to you, line by line, how knowing your rights will change your life.

- ***License and registration and step out of the car.***

  The police ask for your paperwork. Give it to them as you are stepping out the car. Make sure your car is locked. All they can do is pat you down.

- ***Are you carrying a weapon on you? I know a lot of you are / I ain't stepping out of shit, all my papers legit***

  You don't have to answer their questions, but you are breaking the law by not following the police order to step out the car. It is extremely dangerous not to because the cops might be scared of you and you don't want any problems.

- ***Well, do you mind if I look around the car a little bit?***

  You don't have the right to look in my car, so the answer is ***NO***.

- ***Well, my glove compartment is locked, so is the trunk in the back / And I know my rights, so you're going need a warrant for that.***

I know you need a warrant to search me and my car, and just to let you know, I did lock it, so you don't try to break in or frame me.

Once you give your consent to be searched, an attorney cannot help you get the charge thrown out in court!

I tell people all the time it's harder to break the law than it is just to follow it, but I realize that may not always be true. The fact that you go to school or work every day and just go home doesn't mean that somewhere between the two you didn't do something wrong. No matter how small it may seem—*for example,* you didn't put on your seatbelt—it is still breaking the law. No matter how big or small it is, all it takes is one police officer who's having a bad day to pull you over, and you, ***Mr. or Ms. I Don't Break the Law,*** could end up in jail.

They're constantly out here looking for people who are breaking the law. In agencies where they don't have quotas, if an officer works an 8-to-12-hour shift, how can they justify that there hasn't been anyone breaking the law the whole time they were working? Or, were they *really* working? Most officers aren't out there trying to hem you up. However, if you get pulled over and don't get a ticket, but you get a warning, you need to know the warning is recorded. So, if you get pulled over again and you're asked about your driving record, tell the truth. If they check, they will see you have been pulled over previously, but if you're honest, they have the discretion to let you slide again.

Which brings me to, when you're driving and the police are behind you, they generally run your license plate. That will tell them to whom the car is registered, and in many states, if you have insurance. So, it is pointless to give a false name when you get pulled over. "Why?" you ask. In most states, the police system is connected to the Secretary of State's system (or DMV in some states) and they get your picture. Not to mention, you are being recorded, and lying is a charge of resisting and obstructing justice.

Also, it is important to know, if you have unpaid tickets, a Warrant could have been issued for you even if you are a minor. If so, they have the right to arrest you. By law, they are supposed to arrest anyone with a Warrant. What you need to know about Warrants is, once you've been arrested, you can be held for up to 72 hours. Depending on what city the Warrant was issued in, however, there is a radius on the area you can be picked up. What that means is, let's say the Warrant was issued in Detroit, Michigan, and there's a 30-mile-radius pick up. If you're stopped 60 miles from Detroit, the city in which you were stopped can let you go because they don't have to pick you up. What you need to do after that is make sure you try to take care of that ticket because it can come back to haunt you later.

If you're arrested, you'll be able to use the phone and make more than one call. You need to know people's telephone numbers because you will not be able to have your cellphone. You also need to know most cellphones are not setup for collect calls, so you may want to know someone's house (landline) phone number.

Even though you are a minor, you and your parents need to pay attention to what happens when dealing with the courts and attorneys. You think and hope your attorney is doing the right thing and fighting for your case for you in the best way possible, but if you think something isn't right, remember to do your own research because ***NO*** attorney is going to tell you they messed up your case and that's why you're getting locked up. ***NO*** police officer is going to say they may have made a mistake and lied on you to get you locked up. So, you need to watch your own back and pay attention to what is said because it's your life and you may have to be the one to save it. Plus, if they did something wrong, you and your parents need to know how to research the law to get your case overturned and maybe get a new trial.

A. Tips For When You're Pulled Over, Even If You're On A Bike Or Just Walking

(1) ***Never flee.*** You will get caught and it will only make the situation worse.

(2) You need to understand that driving with a suspended license or maybe a bag of marijuana in your car is not worth getting a felony fleeing case.

(3) When you know your rights in the first place, they have no right to search your car. They can pat you down but not go in your pockets or purse.

(4) ***Be nice, even if you're mad!***

(5) Everything is recorded, so don't just start talking or answering questions.

(6) Put both hands on the steering wheel.

(7) Ask the officer why you were pulled over.

(8) ***Then, be quiet!***

(9) Try not to get tricked into admitting you did something wrong—things like you didn't have your seatbelt on or you were speeding.

(10) Make sure your door is locked.

(11) Cracking your window gives them less chance to smell marijuana, so they can't use the fact they smelled marijuana to search your car.

(12) If you don't have insurance or the registration, say you misplaced it. Then take the ticket and resolve it later.

(13) If they ask to search your car, ask why, then say, ***"I DO NOT GIVE CONSENT!"*** You may have to repeat it a few times as they may try bully you.

(14) Ask if you're being detained or if you're free to go.

(15) If you have to get out the car: Turn the car off, take the keys out the ignition, put the keys in your pocket, and ask the officer to step away from your car. Lock the door as you are getting out and shut the door. They still have no right to search you or your car. And, yes, they are trying to think of a reason to get into your car.

Note: If you have keyless operation, make sure you put your keys in your pocket before the cop gets to your car. If you're a woman, you don't want to go to reach for your keys from your purse, for instance, and the officer mistakes it for something else.

(16) Don't forget to ask the officer if you're free to go or if you're being detained.

(17) If you are arrested and there's a licensed passenger in your vehicle, the police can let them take your vehicle instead of impounding it. ***Beware:*** the police like to impound your vehicle so they can do an inventory search. That gives them the right to look through your vehicle. That's their way of getting around a Warrant.

(18) If you are alone if you are arrested and you locked your car when you got out of it, they may just let someone come pick it up instead of impounding it.

(19) Keep your doors locked because the police may try to open the door without you wanting them to.

(20) Don't fall for the set up. If you only roll your window down a little bit, it gives them less reason to say they need to search your car because they claim they smell marijuana, and it's for your own safety. Plus, it shows them you know your rights, and they can't just reach in your car and open your door.

(21) The first thing you need to ask the officer is why you were pulled over. For example, if they say you were speeding, that only gives them Probable Cause to get your license, registration, and insurance. Nothing else!

(22) Ask the officer if you have committed a crime. At this point, the crime is only going to get you a ticket. The officer has no probable cause to search you. It's the 4th Amendment.

(23) Even if you don't have proof of insurance with you, that doesn't give them the right to search you.

(24) There is no legal basis for your passengers to have to give them their identification, even if they ask for it.

(25) Most people make the mistake of giving the officer permission to search their car. You do not have to give the officer permission to search your car.

(26) There's a difference between permission and Probable Cause. Don't get tricked into letting an officer search your car. Don't give them an opportunity to put something in your car.

(27) Also, you do not have to answer any questions. *For example,* if the officer asks where you're going, tell the officer you don't have to answer that.

(28) If you're asked to get out the car, you have to get out the car or you can get arrested for disobeying a lawful order. But that doesn't give them the right to search you by going through your pockets. They can only pat you down.

***

21. You Have Rights

A. Never give the police permission to search your car, even if you have nothing in it at all. The police have to show a reason to search and question you, but ***if you consent***, they do not need a reason.

B. If you consent, you have just given your rights away. Consent is the enemy of your constitutional rights. Don't assume the cops are justified in searching or questioning you, so you just agree to give consent. If they were justified, they wouldn't ask for your consent.

C. Don't be intimidated by the cop telling you it will go easier for you if you give consent. It goes easier for them, not you!

D. If they want to look through your car, in your purse, in your trunk, etc., ***do not give your consent!*** Do you mind opening your trunk? Open your purse. These are all ways the cops get consent.

E. The cops will not tell you they need consent to look. They ask for it in sneaky ways so you don't even realize what you just did. They may threaten to arrest you and impound your car if you don't consent. That is unjust and inconvenient. There is no crime on insisting on your constitutional rights, and there is no crime in not consenting.

F. Another way to give your rights away is when the police ask you to come in for questioning. This is voluntary. Even if you feel intimidated that you need to go, you don't have to.

G. Please know they have no rights unless you are taken into custody and that usually means an arrest.

H. Do you think when you are in a police car that the police stop recording? They don't, and everything you say will be used against you! That's why it is important at all times to use you rights and stay silent.

I. If you start talking to the cops without them asking you a direct question, you have just given your rights up, even if you are in custody!

J. If the cops are talking amongst themselves or to someone else and you overhear them (this is intentional on their part), you may feel the need to chime in. You just gave away your rights, even if you are in custody!

K. ***If you wish to remain silent, you must remain silent! If you talk, you have just given up your rights!***

L. If they ask to search your car, even if: (a) you think they will find it or see it, (b) you think you have nothing to hide, (c) you think saying ***no*** *will* get you in more trouble, or (d) worse, you think they'll search no matter what you say, ***always say no!***

M. The cops may try to coerce you by telling you that you'll get in more trouble by saying no or that it will go harder on you if they have to get a Warrant, etc. If you give your consent, you have just given up your constitutional rights.

N. If you give your consent, the cops don't need Probably Cause to search. If you don't give your consent, then the cops have to give the court a good reason why they searched your vehicle. So, if you are a minor, never give them consent. Call your parents.

O. The same goes for a pat-down search. If a cop sees you on the street, they have to have Reasonable Suspicion that you committed a crime. Then they can only ask your name (you need to tell the truth if you decide to answer) and they can only pat you down for what they can readily feel through your clothing. This is not an invasive search. ***Unless you give them consent!***

P. The cops can get away with more than a pat-down if you tell on yourself. If the cop asks what are you carrying and you tell him, then you've just told on yourself. Even if it's something that has nothing to do with the crime the cop had suspicions about in the first place, or if it's something they never would have detected by a pat-down search, you just told on yourself and gave away your rights!

Q. You cannot disobey a lawful order from a police officer—*for example:* if the police officer asks you to get out the car. Failure to obey a lawful order is a felony.

R. You ***ARE NOT*** going to win a fight with the cops on the street. They have power and force. Be polite and comply with all direct orders, but do not give consent if asked and remain silent. The fight comes later in the courtroom. One ugly charge that can be added to a minor infraction is resisting and obstructing a police officer, which is a felony.

S. You can always make complaints about people, even the police. You can go to different departments, *for example,* if it's the City police, complain to the State police about them. Keep complaining until someone listens. Don't take no or indifference for an answer.

T. Make sure you Google what Motions are so you can keep an eye on your attorney. Filing the right Motions can win your case.

***

22. Charge Glossary

A. First Degree Criminal Sexual Conduct (CSC 1)

- Vaginal, oral, or anal sex, actual insertion, sex with a minor, or sex with the mentally challenged.
- Penalty: Life in a state prison, possible life without parole, possible minimum 25 years, lifetime GPS tether.
- Sex Offender Registration: Lifetime public registration, quarterly reporting.

B. Second Degree Criminal Sexual Conduct (CSC 2)

- Touching with sexual satisfaction. Rubbing penis on a clitoris without insertion and ejaculation.
- Penalty: 15 years in a state prison, possible lifetime GPS tether.
- Sex Offender Registration: Lifetime or 25 years public registration, quarterly or semi-annual reporting.

C. Third Degree Criminal Sexual Conduct (CSC 3)

- Penetration (fingering), possibly consensual but underage.
- Penalty: 15 years in a state prison.
- Sex Offender Registration: Lifetime public registration, quarterly reporting.

D. Fourth Degree Criminal Sexual Conduct (CSC 4)

- Touching someone in an inappropriate sexual way (grabbing breasts, butt, or crotch).
- Penalty: 2 years in a state prison and/or $500 fine.

- Sex Offender Registration: Lifetime, 25, or 15 years public registration (depending on age of Complainant), quarterly, semi-annual, or annual reporting.

E. Assault With Intent To Commit Criminal Sexual Conduct Involving Sexual Penetration

- Assault, planning to actually have sex (holding someone down, but not actually finishing).
- Penalty: 10 years in a state prison.
- Sex Offender Registration: Lifetime public registration, quarterly reporting.

F. Assault With Intent To Commit Criminal Sexual Conduct In The Second Degree

- Assault, planning to orgasm (by masturbation).
- Penalty: 5 years in a state prison.
- Sex Offender Registration: Lifetime, 25, or 15 years public registration (depending on age of Complainant), quarterly, semi-annual, or annual reporting.

G. Accosting, Enticing, or Soliciting a Child for Immoral Purposes (Accosting a Minor for Immoral Purposes)

- Bribe or make a promise to a child for sex.
- Penalty: 4 years in a state prison and/or $4,000 fine.
- Sex Offender Registration: 25 years public registration, semi-annual reporting.

H. Gross Indecency

- Sexual acts between the same gender.
- Penalty: 5 years in a state prison and/or $2,500 fine; minimum 1 day in jail and maximum life in a state prison for "sexually delinquent persons".
- Sex Offender Registration: Lifetime or 25 years public registration (depending on ages of Complainant and accused), quarterly or semi-annual reporting.

I. Child Sexually Abusive Material (and Child Sexually Abusive Activity)

- Child naked pictures or video.
- Penalty: 4, 7, 0r 20 years in a state prison and/or a $10,000, $50,000, or $100,000 fine, respectively, depending on whether the alleged offense involves knowing possession, distribution, or production of the child sexually abusive material.
- Sex Offender Registration: 25 or 15 years public registration, annual or semi-annual reporting.

J. Indecent Exposure & Aggravated Indecent Exposure

- Showing your private parts.
- Penalty: 1 year in jail and/or a $1,000 fine (Indecent Exposure); 2 years in a state prison and/or a $2,000 fine (Aggravated Indecent Exposure).
- Sex Offender Registration: Possible 15 years public registration.

K. Felonious Assault (Assault With a Dangerous Weapon)

- Attacking a person with a weapon.
- Penalty: 4 years in a state prison and/or $2,000 fine.

L. Assaulting, Resisting, Or Obstructing A Police Officer ("Certain Persons")

- Lying to the police, not following the police's directions, or resisting the police.
- Penalty: 2 years in a state prison and/or $2,000 fine.

M. Felony Domestic Violence, Third Offense

- Injure a spouse or person in same house (most likely your 3rd time).
- Penalty: 5 years in a state prison and/or $5,000 fine.

N. Assault With Intent To Do Great Bodily Harm ("GBH"), Less Than Murder

- Serious injury causing harm to a person's health.
- Penalty: 10 years in a state prison and/or $5,000 fine.

O. Assault With Intent To Commit Murder ("AWICM")

- Not just assaulting a person, but trying to kill, not just hurt, a person.
- Penalty: Life in a state prison or any term of years.

P. Assault With Intent To Commit A Felony (Other Various Types)

- Michigan law has also earmarked certain felonies for special treatment with specific statutes, including even harsher potential punishment. Here are a few examples:
- ♦ Assault With Intent to Commit Armed Robbery: Life in a state prison.
- ♦ Assault With Intent to Commit Unarmed Robbery: 15 years in a state prison.
- ♦ Assault With Intent to Commit Sexual Penetration: 10 years in a state prison.
- ♦ Assault With Intent to Commit Sexual Contact: 5 years in a state prison.
- ♦ Assault With Intent to Maim: 10 years in a state prison.

Q. Stalking

- Always watching someone or always contacting someone who doesn't want to be contacted by you. You're obsessed.
- Penalty: 1 year in jail and/or $1,000 fine, or 5 years in a state prison and a $10,000 fine (depending on the circumstances).

R. Aggravated Stalking

- Threatening and harassing while always watching someone.
- Penalty: 5 years in a state prison and/or $10,000 fine, or 10 years in a state prison and a $15,000 fine (depending on the circumstances).

S. Domestic Assault, First Offense

- Assaulting someone you're in a relationship with.
- Penalty: 93 days in jail and/or $500 fine, or both.

T. Domestic Assault, Second Offense

- Second time assaulting someone you're in a relationship with.
- Penalty: 1 year in jail and/or $1,000 fine, or both.

U. Aggravated Domestic Assault

- Assault of the person you're in a relationship with that would cause serious injury.
- Penalty: 1 year in jail and/or $1,000 fine, or both.

V. Domestic Assault, Third Offense – Felony

- Third time assaulting a spouse with injury.
- Penalty: 5 years in a state prison and/or $5,000 fine, or both.

W. First Degree Home Invasion

- Someone breaks into and enters a home with intent to steal or assault; or breaks and enters a dwelling without permission, and at any time during the breaking and entering, they steal or assault and are armed with a dangerous weapon; or another person is lawfully in the dwelling at the time of the breaking and entering. 20 years.

X. Second Degree Home Invasion

- Someone breaks into and enters a home with intent to steal or assault; or someone enters without permission to commit felony larceny or assault; or someone breaks and enters without permission, and during the breaking and entering, commits a felony, larceny, or assault. 15 years.

Y. Third Degree Home Invasion

- Someone breaks into a home with intent to steal. 5 years.
- Someone breaks into and enters a building with intent to commit a misdemeanor in the building, enters without permission with intent to commit a misdemeanor in the building; or breaks and enters without permission, and during the breaking and entering, commits a misdemeanor. 2-5 years.
- Someone breaks into and enters a building without permission, and at any time while entering the building, present in the building, or exiting the building, violates any of the following: an order to protect a person or persons; a probation term or condition; a parole term or condition; a personal protection order term or condition; a bond or bail condition; or a pretrial release condition. 2-5 years

Z. First Degree Retail Fraud (Felony)

- Intent to steal from a store. Jail time of up to 5 years and potential fine of either $10,000 or three times the value of the stolen property, whichever is greater.

AA. Second Degree Retail Fraud (Misdemeanor)

- Jail time of up to 1 year and a potential fine of either $2,000 or three times the value of the stolen property, whichever is greater.

AB. Third Degree Retail Fraud (Misdemeanor)

- Jail time of up to 93 days and a potential fine of either $500 or three times the value of the stolen property, whichever is greater.

AC. Carrying a Concealed Weapon (CCW)

- Carrying a firearm or dangerous weapon (dagger, dirk, razor, stiletto, taser, or knife having a blade over 3 inches in length). 2-5 years.

***

23. Life Skills

When you are dealing with the real world, there are reasons you must know what you are doing. Everyone wants something from you. We are made to look out for ourselves. It's called surviving. The better you can adapt to any situation, the better off you will be. You just have to pay attention to what is being said and done around you.

For example: When you are around good people, they generally are trying to do things that will make themselves better. They plan, then do. If you hang around them, you will try to find ways to make your situation better. But, if you are around shady people, you will find shortcuts to do things quickly instead of taking your time and doing things the right way. It's a right-now decision that generally doesn't work in the long run because you didn't have a plan.

People may promise you things, then don't follow through. You need to be prepared to do for yourself what they promised you, or you're going to have to find another way to get it done. There is always more than one way to do something. You have to think outside the box. Talk to other people to find another way because you can only depend on yourself.

Do you know how to prepare yourself for the ups and downs?

There are a lot of people who do not have self-esteem, so they will try to make *you* feel bad or bully you. Your job is to recognize that they don't have good intentions for you and get away from them. Whatever their issues are, you don't want any part of them. You have better things to do with yourself.

Decisions are important because if you make the wrong one, you can get in trouble. And when you get in trouble, you're the one who's going to have to pay the price. If you break the law, you're the one who's going to jail. Even if you broke the law with others, it's your life that's on the line. So, you need to realize what you do in any situation will affect you and your life.

People who do a lot of positive things are generally more successful. You can't think things are going to work out for you without putting the work in. Most people realize that having connections and networking is a game, and to succeed, you need help. That help is called allies. These are the people who will stand up for you and say good things about you. The only thing you need to know is to make sure you don't put your allies in a bad situation because they may have to make a decision that may not benefit you.

EVERYONE IS NOT YOUR FRIEND! There are people out here who just want to see you fail and get into trouble. What you have to look out for with these types of people is they sometimes try to act like they are your friends. They give you small signs that you tend to overlook. You will find yourself making excuses for what they did. That is a red flag for you leave them alone. Never make excuses for people. They did what they wanted to do; let them stand on it. If someone slaps you in the face, are you going to stick around for them to do it again? No! You know they wanted to do it, even if they say they're sorry, and you need to get away from them. See, the haters and backstabbers always have something up.

Even though people are not from where you may be from doesn't give them the right to look down on you and think or act like they are better than you. Your life and situations make you who you are, and it is up to you to show that. *For example:* Someone grew up in a two-parent home and both parents work. Yes, they may have had a better start than you, but now is the time for you to start making the changes to give yourself a better chance at succeeding. You may know some things they don't know. Like, you were raised in a house where there were drugs and partying, perhaps your parents were on drugs, and your family or a friend is raising you. You may be able to spot a drug dealer quickly or a con artist. You may learn faster that you can't trust or tell everyone everything, so you start developing skills that some of these other people won't until later in life.

Use what you have to get what you want. You may have a skill of learning how to adapt and to work hard because you've had to. Maybe your parent(s) isn't good with money; the bills aren't getting paid and things are getting turned off. You need to understand how money works at an early age so you won't go through what they are. Learn to balance a checkbook or negotiate with the phone company to not shut off your phone and to get an extension by calling instead of letting it just get turned off. You have the skills you need, so use them. Even though they may be a step above you, work hard and outmaneuver them. Then you will win!

Most of the time, companies hire people who look good on paper. What that means is their education and résumés say exactly what they are looking for. Or, maybe they have a hook-up at the job—you know, maybe their family or a friend works there. But a lot of times, these people may be the wrong people for the job. There are people who will not understand your situation, where you came from. They will judge you without even knowing anything about you. They will be your boss, your teacher, and generally, someone who can help you, but they choose not to because they have some type of issue within themselves. You cannot worry about these horrible, low-self-esteem, over-educated people who don't have common sense and whose values and morals may be questionable. You need to move on and find another way. That may not be the right situation for you.

Learn when to move on or you will lose every time. Learn how to trust yourself. When something doesn't look right or add up, it isn't, so stay away from it. You have to protect yourself.

As a minor, how long do you think you will be able to live off your parents once you become an adult? Once you become of age, they no longer have to feed you, clothe you, or let you live with them, so don't you think it is important to start making plans to survive on your own? Do you even know the things you will need to survive on your own? *For example:* Do you know you aren't supposed to give your social security number to just anyone because they can steal your identification? Or, what happens if you lose your identification? Did you know you have to go to the Secretary of State and give them 2 forms of identification to replace it? You can use a birth certificate, a school ID, a yearbook picture, or perhaps some mail.

Whatever you want in life, you must work for it. It can be hard, but just don't stop. There's an old saying: Anything worth having is worth working for!

24. *Identification, Bank Accounts, And Driving/Insurance Laws*

You need to have an identification, a bank account. The identification tells who you are and where you live, like a driver's license or a State-issued ID. A bank account is a second form of contact and identity. Also, you can't build credit and have access to loans and other monies without a bank account. It also shows, that if you burn too many banks (for example, unpaid overdrafts), you are not good with money or trustworthy. Yes, you can go to small banks that don't use check systems as a background check, but everyone needs a bank account. Plus, if you don't have a bank account and have to cash check, stores and check cashing places will overcharge you.

You need a driver's license to show you know the rules and were taught how to responsibly drive an automobile. We are not playing GTA (Grand Theft Auto); this is real life. Stealing cars, killing people, and doing some really dangerous crimes in a game is one thing, but having an accident, outrunning the police, and other crimes in real life will change your life forever. People need to know the difference.

Youths and adults don't have as much conversation as they use to have before all the social media and technology, but it is both the youths' and the parents' responsibility to have discussions on all the rules and information in this book so you don't get into trouble. Some parents try hard to keep their kids away from all the bad things in life, but if you don't discuss them, you may make the wrong decision or might not even recognize it's trouble. There are many unspoken rules when driving that many people don't know until they get pulled over, so let's see what you know and have been through.

1. Have you ever been pulled over by the police? ______________________________
2. Have you ever been in a car with someone when they were being pulled over?

   ____
3. Have you ever seen someone get pulled over? ______________________________
4. What is required when you are pulled over by the police? ____________________

   ____

   ____
5. What is car insurance? ____
6. What does car insurance do? ____

   ____

   ____

7. How long is car insurance good for? ______________________

8. What is proof of registration? ______________________

____

9. How long is registration good for? ______________________

10. Before driving someone's car should you ask if it is insured and registered? ______

11. Have you driven a car that was not properly registered? ______________________

12. Have you driven a car that had no insurance? ______________________

13. Have you driven a car without a driver's license or permit? ______________________

14. What do you think of when you see a person being pulled over? ______________________

____

____

15. Have you ever rode in a car with someone didn't have a driver's license? __________

16. Have you ever rode with someone whose car was not registered? ______________________

17. Have you ever been in the car with someone who was pulled over who didn't have insurance? ______________________

____

18. Can the police pull you over and demand you immediately get out of the car?

____

19. Are you scared of being pulled over by the police? ______________________

20. Have you been pulled over with someone who had a gun in the car? ______________________

21. What is your mood when you get pulled over? ______________________

22. How is you attitude when you get pulled over? ______________________

23. If you know you are being profiled and pulled over, how do you behave?

____

____

____

A. Sticky Situation Scenarios

1. When being pulled over what is the first thing you need to do? ____________

2. What do you need to give an officer when pulled over? ____________

3. How far do you need to roll your window down? ____________

4. What if you have tinted windows? ____________

5. Do you need to keep your doors locked? ____________

6. How long do the police have to bring a dog to sniff around your car?

7. What is a civil infraction, a misdemeanor, a felony? ____________

8. If an officer asks you do you know why I pulled you over, you say? ____________

9. What do you do if an officer refuses to tell you why they pulled you over?

10. When an officer asks you where you are going, what do you say? ____________

11. Why is it important for you to find out why the officer pulled you over? ___

12. When do the police cameras start recording when they pull someone over? ___

13. If an officer sees you breaking the law, then turns on his lights, will you win in court? ___

14. Can an officer search your car when they ask you to get out the car? ___

15. What is probable cause and in plain sight? ___

16. How can the police search your person? ___

17. Can you be arrested if your passenger is smoking marijuana when you're driving? ___

18. If you don't have a driver's license on your person when pulled over, can you be arrested? ___

19. If an officer asks you where you're going, what do you say? ___

20. If you've never had a driver's license, can you be arrested? ___

21. If you forgot your license at home, where can you find your driver's license number? ___

22. If your license is suspended, can you be arrested? ___

23. If your license is suspended, can your car be searched and towed? ___

24. If you don't have insurance, can your car be searched? ___

25. If you don't have insurance, can you be arrested? ____________
26. Can your car be towed if you don't have insurance? ____________
27. Can the officer see in the system if you have insurance? ____________
28. If your don't have insurance, what do you tell the officer? ____________

____

____

29. If you can't afford insurance, what can you do? ____________

____

____

30. If your car is not registered, can you be arrested? ____________
31. If your car is not properly registered, can it be towed? ____________
32. If your car is not properly registered can it be searched? ____________
33. If you buy another car and put the old license plate on that car, can you be arrested? ____________
34. If the license plate from the other car is on your car, can your car be towed?

____

35. If you have attitude and say you're DWB, can you get a ticket? ____________
36. Can you smoke marijuana in your car? ____________
37. Can you be under the influence of drugs in public? ____________
38. Can you open-carry in your car? ____________
39. Can you sit in a car with a loaded gun? ____________
40. Can you carry a loaded gun outside your vehicle? ____________
41. Can you file a complaint against the police? ____________
42. Can you sue a police officer personally? ____________
43. If so, what can you sue a police officer for? ____________

____

44. How do you end the police stop quickly? ____________

____

____

____

25. The 27 Amendments To The Constitution

Below is a list of the *27 Amendments to the Constitution*. Under each, write what you think it means.

A. 27 Amendments To The Constitution—Summarized

1791 Bill of Rights (First Ten Amendments)

1st Freedom of Speech, Press, Religion, Assembly and Petition.

____

____

____

2nd Right to bear arms.

____

____

____

3rd Right to not quarter soldiers in your home without permission.

____

____

____

4th Freedom from unlawful search and seizure without probable cause.

____

____

____

5th Right to due process, right not to incriminate yourself, law of eminent domain. Double Jeopardy.

____

____

____

6th Right to a fair and speedy trial, right to know the charges against you, right to a lawyer, right to face your accuser.

____

____

____

7th Right to a jury trial in civil cases.

____

____

____

8th No excessive bail/ fines nor or unusual punishment.

9th Unenumerated rights.

10th Powers reserved to the states.

11th States cannot be sued in federal court by other states or foreign countries (1794).

12th Election of both President & vice-president together (not separately) (1803).

13th Abolition of slavery (1865).

14th Repeals 3/5ths compromise and makes all people of the U. S. Citizen (1868).

15th Right to vote for citizens (but NOT guaranteed to anyone only that states cannot discriminate (1870)).

16th Federal income tax provision (1913).

17th Senators to be elected by voters of the state (1913).

18th Prohibition (outlawed all aspects of alcohol EXCEPT drinking it) (1919).

19th Right to vote for women (1920).

20th Date of inauguration of president moved from March to January following November election (1933).

21st Repeals 18th amendment (1933).

22nd Tenure of President: no president may serve more than two terms (1951).

23rd D.C. allowed to have their own electors (1961).

24th No "tax" in order to vote (1964).

25th Allows for presidential succession (1967).

26th Right to vote minimum age 18 (1971).

____

____

____

27th Congress may not vote themselves a pay raise until after the next election (1992).

____

____

____

B. 27 Amendments To The Constitution—Expounded

1. Guarantees freedom of speech, religion, and press, and the right to assemble peaceably and petition the government for redress of grievances (to ask it to fix something that it's responsible for).
2. The belief was strong that a well-regulated militia (such as the National Guard, in modern times) was necessary for maintaining our national security, so the political leaders in Congress guaranteed that the right to bear arms would not be infringed (violated).
3. No soldier in time of peace shall be quartered in a private citizen's home without the homeowner's consent.
4. People and their personal property cannot be searched without a warrant, issued by a judge.
5. No person may be held to answer for a crime unless he or she has first been officially and legally charged (through an indictment by a grand jury or a presentment from a prosecutor). No person can be tried for a crime, found not guilty, then tried again for that same exact crime. (Double jeopardy is the term used in law. Double jeopardy is forbidden by this amendment.) Persons cannot be deprived of life, liberty, or property, without due process of law. Private property cannot be taken for public use unless the owner is fairly compensated for it.
6. A person accused of a crime has the right to a fair and speedy trial by an impartial jury of his/her peers, to be informed of the accusations against him/her, to be confronted with the witnesses against him/her, to be able to subpoena (summon) witnesses to give testimony in his/her favor, and to have legal counsel (an attorney) for his/her defense.
7. In any legal case involving a civil suit (lawsuit between two persons or groups), the defendant has the right to a trial by jury if the amount in question is over twenty dollars.
8. No excessive bail or fines, or cruel and unusual punishment shall be used against a convicted criminal.

9. No one shall be denied their basic constitutional rights.
10. Powers that are not specifically granted to the national government are to be retained by the states and people.
11. A citizen from one state cannot sue a citizen in another state in federal court.
12. Presidential Electors will vote for President and Vice President on separate ballots.
13. Involuntary servitude—slavery—was abolished, unless it was the result of a sentence passed by a court of law upon conviction of a crime.
14. This is the basic guarantee of civil rights for all Americans. It defined "citizenship" as anyone born or naturalized in the U.S. (this automatically granted citizenship rights to former slaves). States were prohibited from enforcing any law that took away the rights, privileges, and immunities guaranteed to U.S. citizens without first making certain that "due process of law" had been carried out. All persons were now guaranteed "equal protection of the laws," regardless of who they were or what their race, religion, or country of origin happened to be. No person who served in the government of the southern confederacy during the Civil War was allowed to hold federal office. The U.S. government refused to accept any debts incurred by the Confederate States of America, including claims for the loss or emancipation of any slave.
15. African American males were guaranteed the right to vote, and "race, color, or previous condition of servitude" could not be used as a reason to refuse anyone the right to vote.
16. Congress shall have the power to levy and collect taxes on incomes.
17. Election of Senators was granted to the people of each of the states.
18. The manufacture, transportation or sale of alcoholic beverages was prohibited.
19. The right to vote cannot be denied because of a person's sex.
20. Shortened the period of time between federal elections (first week of November in even numbered years) and the day that officials were sworn into office. Called the "Lame Duck Amendment" because it gave "lame duck" officials (those who were not going to be sworn in, but were still in office) a shorter period of time to pass laws that tended to enrich their lives or the lives of their friends and political allies. Presidential inauguration day (when he/she is sworn in) moved back from March 4 to January 20. Members of Congress are now sworn into office on January 3 instead of March 4 of odd numbered years.
21. Repealed a previously-ratified amendment; the Prohibition Era in America was over.

22. President of the U.S. now limited to serving no more than two terms in office, and no more than a total of ten years (in the case where a Vice President moves into the presidency as the result of a vacancy in that office, and is re-elected to his/her own terms of office).
23. People who live in Washington, D.C. are allowed to vote for President and granted three electoral votes, the minimum number of Electoral College ballots. (Before this amendment, residents of the District of Columbia were prohibited from voting for President.)
24. People cannot be denied the right to vote in federal elections – either primaries or general elections – because they have not paid a tax on voting. (Before this amendment, poor people, and most particularly ethnic and racial minorities, were effectively kept from voting by such "poll taxes" that they simply could not afford to pay. This prohibition on poll taxes was later extended to state and local elections, as well.)
25. Established procedures to follow in the case of presidential death and/or disability. States for the first time in the Constitution that the Vice President, when taking over the office of President after a vacancy occurs, has all of the powers and responsibilities of the presidency. In case of presidential disability, the Vice President and a majority of his/her Cabinet officers may send written notice to the Speaker of the House of Representatives and the President Pro Tempore of the Senate that the President of the U.S. is "unable to discharge his duties and responsibilities," the Vice President becomes Acting President. When the President is able to resume the duties that his office requires, he may send written notice to the congressional leadership that he is returning to his office. If the Vice President and a majority of the Cabinet officers disagree, they may send written notice to the leaders of Congress. Congress will then decide who should take office as President.
26. Established the minimum age requirement for voting in federal elections at eighteen years.
27. Congress may pass a law increasing their salaries, but cannot collect it until after there has been a federal election.

***

26. Know Your Rights (Retest)

A. Rights That Apply To Minors

Minors do have legal rights. You have the right to equal protection. You have the right to due process, to have your day in court, an education, basic needs, health care, good nutrition, and a safe environment.

(1) *The 1st Amendment. Freedom of Speech, Religion, Press, Assembly & Petition.*

You have the right to:

- *Say what you want without causing a dangerous situation.*
- *Believe in whatever religion you want—or don't believe in one at all—your choice.*
- *Write what you want, just not on other people's property.*
- *Disagree with the government and sue them.*

There are rules on freedom of speech. For example, you can't yell something like fire in a public place because it could cause people to panic, causing a dangerous situation.

(a) *If the police stop you and ask you a question, do you have to answer? If so, what do you have to tell them?* ______________________

____

____

____

____

(b) *What can happen if you curse at the police?* ______________

____

____

____

(c) *Do you have to pray or stand for the national anthem (in schools or in public)?*

____

____

(d) *Can you write or draw on anything, anywhere?* ______________

____

____

(e) *Do you have the right to hang out in a group?* ______________

____

(f) *Do you have the right to not like a rule the government makes?* ______

____

(g) *What's the procedure to try to change the rules without getting punished by the government?* ____________________

____

____

____

(h) *Can a minor sue the government?* ____________________

(i) *Can you get sued as a minor?* ____________________

(2) *The 2nd Amendment. The Right to Bear Arms*

If you are of legal age, you have the right to have a weapon and use it to protect yourself.

(a) *Can you carry a weapon just to protect yourself? If so, what kind of weapon?*

____

____

____

(3) *The 4th Amendment. Search and Seizure*

The government cannot arrest you or search your property unless they have Probable Cause.

Probable Cause: The police think you have committed a crime or have some type of criminal evidence. It means you are 51% more likely to have done something wrong.

Probable Cause needed for a minor: The police can only search you if they suspect you have violated a criminal statue. However, public officials, like school staff, only need to think you have done something related to a crime.

For example: You keep leaving class, and every time you come back to class, you're acting funny—like you're high or drunk. Then they can pat you down and search your locker.

(a) *If you let the police in your house, can they search it?* ____________________

____

____

(b) *Do you have the right to a phone call? If so, who should you call?*

____

____

(c) *Can cellphones accept collect calls?*

____

(d) *What are Miranda rights?*

____

____

____

____

(e) *Does a minor have Miranda rights?* ____________________

(f) *When should you ask for an attorney—while you're being arrested or after you've been detained?*

____

____

(g) *If the police ignore your request for your parents and attorney, can they keep questioning you? What do you do next?*

____

____

____

(h) *If the police don't tell you your Miranda rights, can you escape punishment?*

____

(i) *What is the number one rule when dealing with the police?*

____

____

***

27. Disclosure

The information given in this guide is true. The place where the crime may be committed may change because of race or gender. The names of the court processes may slightly change because of the court's location.

The *Criminal Chart* is based on first-time offenses. If you have a criminal record, your guidelines for sentencing will be longer prison times. Also, if you have more than one charge, it changes the guidelines and the punishment may be harsher.

Jails are expensive. Inmates get charged $75-$200 per day for "3 hots and a cot". So think about that. Jails charge just as much as a hotel stay, but you didn't ask to stay at their hotel.

THIS WORKBOOK WAS CREATED TO HELP YOU MAKE BETTER CHOICES.

This Workbook is in no way meant to give or replace legal advice. The information herein is provided to help you help yourself, your parents, and your attorney, if you happen to get caught-up in the system!

If you would like tips on getting your case thrown out, to book a seminar, or schedule an appointment, go to the website for help.

If you found this Workbook to be interesting and want additional information, please email me or go to the website and provide your email contact information.

- *Email:* ***banksbailbonds@yahoo.com***
- *Website:* ***stickysituations.info***
- *Instagram:* ***banks_bail_bonds***
- *Facebook:* ***Banks Bail Bonds***

To contact ***Banks Bail Bonds,*** scan the QR code to the left, which will take you directly to the website and the Appendix for this book.

If you purchased this book in eBook format and would like a print copy, you can purchase it from the following sources:

- Directly from me: ***banksbailbonds@yahoo.com***
stickysituations.info
- Our Facebook page: There is a link to purchase the book.

Who says crime doesn't pay? It pays very well—just not for you!

Answers to Quizzes

Know Your Rights (pages 2-5)

(1) *The 1st Amendment. Freedom of Speech, Religion, Press, Assembly & Petition*

(a) *You only have to identify yourself (your name) and show ID.*

(b) *No. If you curse at the police, it is disorderly conduct, which is a misdemeanor, and they have the right to arrest you.*

(c) *No.*

(d) *No. You cannot draw on something that does not belong to you.*

Example: No drawing on a building, which is called graffiti, or you can be charged with vandalism.

There are rules on freedom of the press, like filming and sharing certain negative social media posts on Facebook. That can get you criminally charged. For example, if you ask a minor to take and share a picture of a minor who is naked, you can be charged.

(e) *Yes, as long as it is peaceful.*

(f) *Yes. Everyone has the right to their own opinion. If you don't agree, you can hire a lobbyist (a group of attorneys) to fight and change those laws.*

When you hire a lobbyist, they write laws. Then they give them to Congress to try to get them passed and this is how a bill becomes a law.

Steps:

(i) *A lawyer writes a rule and introduces it to Congress.*
(ii) *Congress reads the rule, then votes. If it passes. it goes to the Senate.*
(iii) *They may have to make some changes and agree on the changes, but once passed and changes are made, it goes to the president to make it a law.*
(iv) *The president can veto it (that means throw it away) or keep it.*
(v) *Congress may veto it also. You need a two-thirds affirmative vote to make it a law and it is a long process.*

(g) *Write a bill to go through Congress so they can vote to make it a law.*

(h) *No.*

(i) *No, but your parents can be sued because of your actions.*

(2) *The 2nd Amendment. The Right to Bear Arms*

(a) *No. There is a difference between having a weapon on you just in case something happens and you need to protect yourself, and carrying a weapon for a reason to harm someone. (If you feel the need to carry a weapon, you and your parents must do the research on what weapons a minor can carry and the rules of carrying that weapon.)*

You can have a weapon, but you can't use it unless you're being attacked.

Example: If you have a gun and someone breaks into your home, you cannot shoot them in the back. If their back is to you, they aren't a threat, so you cannot use your weapon just because you have one.

Even if your parents or a family member has a gun or the right to carry a gun, that does not give you the right to touch or use their gun at any time. If you use this gun, whether you hurt someone or not, you will be charged and so will your parents or family member. It is a felony and a serious crime.

(3) *The 4th Amendment. Search And Seizure*

(a) *Yes. Any time the police come to your house, don't let them inside unless they have a Warrant. Talk through the door. Once you let them inside, they have the right to search your home. This goes for you and adults. If you are a minor, tell the officer to leave his card and you will have your parents call.*

(b) *Yes; your parents and attorney.*

(c) *No, and you should know someone's number who has a landline phone.*

(4) *The 5th Amendment. The Right To Not Self-Incriminate*

(a) *You have the right to remain silent. You have the right to shut up! Don't say anything because it will only get you in more trouble.*

Anything you say can and will be used against you in a court of law. If you do say something, it can and will be used against you later.

You have the right to an attorney. You can protect yourself with an attorney, but you need to shut up until your attorney gets there. You still can get an attorney even if you don't have any money.

Yes.

(b) *Immediately, and stay silent until they show up.*

(c) *They are supposed to stop, but be quiet until your attorney comes.*

(d) *No.*

(e) *Be respectful, especially if you're mad. It can be the difference of life or death.*

Workbook Questionnaire (pages 7-8)

1. c
2. b
3. c
4. e, i, m, n, o, p, q, t
5. a, b, c, f, g, h
6. c
7. c
8. Out of jail.
9. The easiest way for a child to get arrested is because they cannot show identification. By law, they must be able to provide an ID anytime they are outside of their home.
10. 3 years old.
11. You have the right of life, liberty, and property—the rights of the 1st amendment with limitations. For example: You cannot yell something out that will start a riot or chaotic situation.
12. No. Make sure your parents know, if their child is being questioned, they have to agree to you being questioned. No matter the circumstance, they always need an attorney to represent you, no matter how small the question is. This is how people get tricked in the system. Even if you have no money, you still need an attorney to be there. No one makes any statements, no matter how innocent it may seem, **without an attorney present.** It's better not to answer any questions and let you sit for 72 hours because they have to charge you or release you by then. This applies to adults also.
13. Yes. Even though you're a minor, it is still distributing child pornography (the person sending) and a minor in possession of pornography (the person receiving).
14. Yes.
15. Yes. Yes; they can only pat you down for their safety to make sure you don't have any weapons.

True or False Answers
(page 68)

(page 68)

1.	T
2.	T
3.	F
4.	T
5.	F
6.	F
7.	T
8.	T
9.	T
10.	T
11.	T
12.	F
13.	F
14.	T
15.	T
16.	T

Answers to Sticky Situations Scenarios (pages 99-101)

1. Get you phone ready to record. The police can't stop you from recording.
2. Your driver's license, car registration, and proof of insurance.
3. 2 inches, so they can't reach into your car and pull you out.
4. If your tint is dark, roll the window down far enough for them to see your full face.
5. So the police don't just open your door.
6. 15 minutes from the time they pull you over.
7. A civil infraction is a ticket and you cannot be arrested for. A misdemeanor and a felony are crimes for which you can be arrested, like: Operating under the influence or improper plates, both 1 year in jail.
8. You always say NO, because anytime you answer YES, it is admitting guilt.
9. Request a supervisor and wait patiently.
10. You tell them the direction and street you are on (*NICELY*, not sarcastically).
11. Because it can eliminate them having probable cause and the right to search your car.
12. As soon as the officers turn on their lights and siren.
13. Most of the time they don't have the proof, so call the court and request the video.
14. No. They need probable cause. That's why you shut and lock the door when you get out.
15. They think you committed a crime or they see something illegal in your car, like an open alcohol bottle or drugs sitting on the back seat.
16. It is called a pat down. They can only pat you down over your clothes to make sure you are not armed. They CANNOT go into your pockets.
17. Yes. You would be considered driving under the influence. It is a 90-day misdemeanor.
18. Yes, but most of the time, the officer will just give you a ticket or a warning.
19. You politely say what direction you are going in and the street you are on.
20. If you've never applied for a license but drive, yes, you can be arrested, but they normally give you a ticket.
21. On your proof of registration.
22. Yes, that is a 90-day misdemeanor.
23. Yes, searched and towed. If you have a licensed passenger and your car is properly insured and registered, they can give you a break and let them drive your car.

24. No. Not having insurance is a civil infraction which is a ticket, not a reason for probable cause.
25. No. It is a civil infraction. a ticket. Only a misdemeanor or a felony is an arrestable offense.
26. No. That is still a civil infraction.
27. Not always; insurance may be offline. That's why you keep the paperwork in the car.
28. You say you just brought insurance, but you forgot the paperwork at home. Because you can purchase insurance online it back dates by 3 hours.
29. Buy insurance for 1 month. Then put your car in insurance storage; it lasts for 6 months.
30. No. That is a civil infraction, so you will only get a ticket.
31. Yes. It is not supposed to be on driven on the public roads.
32. Yes. If not properly registered, it is required to have an inventory search.
33. Yes. Improper plates is a misdemeanor, up to 1 year in jail.
34. Yes. And an inventory search will be done.
35. Absolutely. By challenging the officer, he must now justify the stop, leading to look for a reason, like a cracked windshield, loud music, broken taillight, your light is out, dark tint, something hanging from window, smell marijuana, etc.
36. Only if your car is in your driveway and there is no key in the ignition.
37. No. You can be charged with disorderly conduct, a misdemeanor.
38. There is no such thing as open-carry in your vehicle. The gun cannot be loaded. The crime is carrying a concealed weapon, a 2-year felony.
39. Only if you have a Concealed Pistol License; that's the license to conceal and carry a loaded gun.
40. As long the gun is visible from 3 views: in front, on the side, and the back, and nothing is covering it. It is called open-carry.
41. Absolutely. Most departments, you can file online, but you can go into the station as well.
42. Absolutely. You can sue them in small claims for up to $5,500 without an attorney.
43. Generally for harassment of defamation of character.
44. Politely ask, "Am I being detained, or am I free to go?"

Notes

Made in United States
Orlando, FL
05 November 2026

90231407R00072